Smarter Than God:

The Case Against Unintelligent Design;
With a brief history of the invention of god

By Oceana Blue

Dedication

This is dedicated to Barbara Marie Hamilton.
Born Feminist.
Devoted Atheist.
Decades, if not centuries ahead of her time.
Lived Feminism before anyone else I knew.
A true original.
Irked the hell out of men.
A true model of appropriate feminine behavior.
She knew what she knew.

Table of Contents

Smarter Than God:

The Case Against Unintelligent Design;

With a brief history of the invention of god

Chapter 1- I'm OK, You're OK, God's not OK

If God's so smart, why is his creation so dumb?
If God's so great, why is his creation so petty?
If God's so kind, why is his creation so cruel?
If God's so good, why is his creation so bad?

It may seem as though I'm overstepping my confidence here, but the following argument basically elucidates how humanity has gotten virtually everything wrong from the very beginning, and how to fix it. In less than 210 pages! Seriously. Ready?

The biggest obstacle to the faith of believers in all three Abrahamic religions (Judaism, Christianity, and Islam) is the Problem of Evil (POE). The problem is a common sense one: evil cannot possibly exist if God is all good and all powerful, as the various religions claim. Yet, evil very clearly *does* exist. It may look different to different people, but nobody would maintain that there is no evil in the world.

So, in order to maintain their cherished faith, religious people find it necessary to come up with an answer to the question, "If God is all good and all powerful, how can there be evil in the world?" because we are definitely going to ask them that. They're going to have a response, it's just going to be incredibly lame. I've presented here a checkmate to their answer, but they aren't going to believe it. You should plant the seed anyway, because occasionally, once in a blue moon, ever so preciously rarely you'll be addressing someone thoughtful enough for it to irritate their mind like a grain of sand in an oyster, and cause a pearl of wisdom to form.

We'll begin with some of the religionists' debate points to convince themselves and each other that god is not a figment of their imagination and collective mental illness.

The primary arguments for the existence of god have to do with creation and design. The basic argument asserts that nothing comes from nothing, so there must be an original creator. This is called the Cosmological argument in the field of Philosophy. Of course, it breaks down when you ask where that creator came from. From nothing? He was just always there? But you just contended that nothing comes from nothing. And like all assertions about the existence of god, when an argument breaks down, the explanation always reverts to magic and faith, no matter how hard the debater is attempting to appear logical, reasonable, and factual.

The current popular argument for the existence of god is that the natural world is too intricate and beautiful to be random, so it must be designed and therefore the designer is god. This is called the Teleological argument in the field of Philosophy, but right now it is being labeled "Intelligent Design" by theists, especially fundamentalist Christians. They proclaim this assertion with a delighted air of "Gotcha", bless their hearts (and I mean that in the Southern way). It is neither logical nor reasonable, and it is not defensible. It, too, falters when asked where the designer came from or who designed the designer. It fails especially when one explicates that this world isn't exactly perfectly, beautifully designed. It has a hell of a lot of flaws which demonstrate their god didn't create the best world by a long shot, and he's a pretty bad designer, as we'll see. If the universe is truly an intelligent design, why is there disease, conflict, and violence? We'll get to that answer shortly.

The Problem of Evil (POE) is the Achilles' heel of Christianity and indeed all monotheistic religions. At least, polytheistic traditions have multiple gods interacting with very human-like behaviors which create interpersonal dramas that explain some of the unpleasant physical and historical phenomena on Earth. They're always getting pissed at each other and kidnapping and killing each other and then the affronted causes an earthquake or volcano or war. Polytheistic tales are regular soap operas, but at least they address the bad things that happen in life.

Maybe monotheism wasn't the upgrade we presume it to be.

That's because going from one ridiculous superstition to another is a lateral move, not an upgrade. It would be like saying those weirdoes over there still believe that stepping on a crack will break the devil's back, but now we sophisticates know that breaking a mirror is seven years of bad luck.

Even Judaism and Islam, while not as invested in the grandiose claim that god is all good and all powerful, have to contend with the question of why a good god (one worthy of our worship) does not use his supposed absolute power to prevent evil. And if Yahweh is not all powerful and all good, why are we worshipping him? Wouldn't he be just a fellow traveler in the universe?

Thousands of dusty, old theologians have spent their entire lives studying and trying to solve the problem of evil. They read the Bible repeatedly, learn ancient, dead languages to better understand and analyze it, write journal articles and books about it, engage in academic exegesis and polemics over it with other fanatics, attend symposia about it, indeed they waste their entire existence trying to figure out how evil can exist if god is all good, and all powerful, attempting desperately to solve the riddle of the Problem of Evil!

All they've come up with, (and what you'll hear from your religious nut debate opponent), after millennia of trying… after all that reading and thinking and learning, all they could manage to scrape together was… the inscrutability defense. The ridiculous and flimsy inscrutability defense asserts that we mere mortals, we lowly humans, we simple country bumpkins are just too unsophisticated and simple to understand god's ways and reasons. We just have to have faith.

Uh oh. This "mere" human female is not too simple and unsophisticated to have god's number. I've cracked the riddle, and I've figured out an irrefutable answer that is the only possible explanation. And boy howdy, folks ain't gonna like it. The answer is, it's the food chain. We have to fix it. Stay with me, now.

The foundational system of god's supposed creation of life is the food chain, the worst possible system, whereby all life depends on death. And not just gentle, welcome eternal rest by natural causes, but almost always heinous, hideous, terrifying, torturous death caused by another, against the will of the one being killed, that is, murder. Except for suicide, all death is murder, be it getting plucked from your pastoral foraging by a raptor and torn alive and eaten, being taken down by a razor-clawed and fanged beast and consumed alive, or languishing in pain from cancer. You don't want to die, but something or someone is overriding your will in the competition for life- murdering you. Not the legal definition, but still violence, pain, suffering and death against your will.

But this is the design god chose for us. In order for a lion to simply survive, a zebra or antelope must suffer the terror and agony of violent murder. In order for humans to live, some think (erroneously), a cow must suffer the terror and torture of the slaughterhouse experience. The only designer who would choose that is a psychopath who loves violence, chaos, competition, destruction and despair, someone who loves the suffering of others. The god that primitive men invented is a psychopath. I will address why men created such an evil god later in the "Brief History of the Invention of god" section, but for now let's discuss the consequences of such a horrible god being passed off as a good, loving god, as we do in, at least, the three major western, Abraham-originated traditions.

If a perfect, all-good, all-intelligent, all-powerful creator made this system whereby survival depends on murder (the food chain) then that normalizes murder and violence. It renders murder and violence acceptable and natural, because that good god ordained it. It is therefore OK to kill. It's OK to kill for food, OK to kill in wars to get resources, territory or just because we don't like others. It's all OK.

How do we expect, then, that individuals should be able to internalize that killing is bad? It's OK to shoot a deer who feels pain and terror and leaves behind family and friends, but somehow it's *not* OK to kill a hunter shooting that deer to make himself feel more powerful, because the hunter would feel terror and pain and leave behind family and friends. And please make no mistake about it: hunters do not kill for food or to control the deer population. They hunt because it makes them feel powerful. I suspect they have very small penises. If it was about population control, it should be open season on the eight fucking billion of us all the time! Of course in American GunWorshipLand, it kind of is.

Violence is god's system. If god is great and violence is his system, then violence must be OK, maybe even great. That justifies all manner of mass shooters, war mongers, physical abusers, murderers and terrorists. They all believe their cause is just and should prevail, so of course they would resort to god's go-to recourse to make their agenda come to pass-- violence. Like the Jan 6th insurrectionists and the 9/11 hijackers (exact same terrorist ilk). Like putin and his war against imaginary nazis in Ukraine. Any crazy cause can be asserted to be holy, to be god's cause.

The food chain proves there is no god. The food chain as a design is ridiculously unintelligent, even evil. It only makes sense as a result of natural selection and evolution. Until we reject the food chain, starting with our position at the top of it, we have no ability, nor moral authority to reject or rebuke any violence. If violence against any sentient being is all right, then violence against all sentient beings, including humans, is apparently all right. What we can do to the other animals, we can do to each other, and have through history- enslaving and torturing enemies, imprisoning people in squalid conditions, even experimenting on other humans, to name but a few.

We draw the line at eating other humans and somehow think that proves our civility. But it's just an arbitrary line that accomplishes nothing but making us feel good about ourselves. We still exploit each other in a variety of ways, making others work for us to make us wealthier, like we do the other animals. We still give other people the bare minimum of sustenance, while keeping the best resources for ourselves, like we do the other animals.

We have definitely used the food chain to rationalize exploitatively taking what we want. We observe that the food chain makes competition for resources the natural order of things and therefore cannot be changed, which means that exploitation is the natural order of things and can never be changed. So... what? *This is the one occasion in which we don't want to fuck with nature? This part of nature we hold sacrosanct, despite our avid advocacy of bending nature to our will in every other circumstance?* It's just an excuse.

Humans love to wax rhapsodic about how perfect a system the food chain is. Even the non-religious love to nibble on that little morsel of anthropomorphist disinformation. But contrary to popular opinion, the food chain is the worst system, guaranteeing an endless cycle of competition, which causes imbalances, shortages, gluts, extinctions, starvation, war, waste and all the phenomena that cause political scientists and economists to tear their hair out, trying to think up ways to correct them.

A snake is plucked from the ground by a hawk, flown to a dizzying height and dropped on a rock to be killed and eaten. A fish is pierced through its mouth with a razor sharp hook and the pain is excruciating. An ant is eaten alive while trapped, struggling in a spider's web. A chipmunk is stalked and snatched, carried into the air and consumed. Can you imagine its terror in the last moment of its life as it helplessly faces its inevitable doom?

Let's try to imagine it with a little thought experiment. You are sitting in your lawn chair enjoying a sunny day and a refreshing beverage. Without warning, you are descended upon by a raptor five times your size and before you even know what's happening, you are pierced through by sharp claws, squeezed tightly like a valuable commodity that must not be dropped, and experience unnatural, uncontrollable, unprotected flight, then you feel a fall and your bones break, but you are still alive and still conscious as your flesh is ripped apart, and a sharp beak bites at you and manages to dislodge a chunk of your body with no regard as to how much your nerve endings feel, before you mercifully die. You know *all* mammals are sentient and have nerve endings, right? This being their usual fate, no wonder squirrels and chipmunks are such godless, little communists!

I doubt that if the people who are so impressed with the exquisite "design" of the food chain were being devoured by a lion or a crocodile, they'd be praising god for his invention of the food chain and thinking to themselves, "Oh, well that's just the food chain for you, a clever system of self-replenishing prey and predators- whoever conceived of it was brilliant!" They'd more likely have as their last thought, "Godfuckingdammit, who's the sick maniac who thought this up?" And an Atheist experiencing being consumed would think, "Damn! The food chain! Wish we'd fixed it!"

Now, Atheists can say, well that's just nature, that's how evolution made it. But they still have to justify all the food chain cruelty they inflict on the other animals in some way, so they resort to something akin to the dominion-over-other-animals argument that religionists use, and took great pains to include in their magic book, the Bible, in the old, original testament. Atheists too contort themselves into pretzels to justify humans' position as apex predators in the food chain: humans are superior; we have those big brains; we have speech, etc, etc, blah, blah, blah ad nauseam.

If the current global trend toward fascist populism, promulgated by petty, racist, sexist, fearful, little men has taught us nothing else, it should demonstrate to us that humans are filthy, stupid animals who are certainly not worthy of dominion over the other animals and plants on Earth. I guarantee you that I know bunnies and deer who are better personalities than the likes of trump and putin.

The monarch of England has dominion over his citizens, who are not even called citizens, but subjects. Yet, if we learned that the king was using his subjects as food and slaves and keeping them in squalid conditions, we would not think that was OK. Yet, there seems to be no boundaries to the horrors we allow ourselves to inflict on other animals under the guise of our dominion over them, who again are sentient beings with personalities (such as the gorilla who gently returned a child who had fallen into her habitat to the zookeeper, carrying him in her arms like a caring Mom, and the otters who put their arms around each other, the giraffe who kisses her baby on the head, etc). If the King decided to have roast peasant for dinner, there would be a major uproar, but roast pheasant is perfectly acceptable. And what if the king hunted peasants for sport, like he might have done to that pheasant? What would our reaction be? Dominion does not automatically convey a right to be cruel (Barbara Hamilton, private conversation, c. 1990).

Make no mistake about it, humans are just animals, mammals, in fact, that bear live offspring, are covered in fur or hair, possessing six major bodily systems: nervous, circulatory, skeletal, digestive, respiratory and reproductive, just like all the other mammals. The same nervous, circulatory and skeletal systems that make it so painful and traumatic for a human to be shot, stabbed or hit by a car, make it just as agonizing for a zebra to be felled by a lion, a chicken or cow to be butchered for food, or a deer to be shot or hit by a car. They understand the fear and pain. They are *terrorized*. It's a specieist (specist?) lie to deny that.

I heard Neal DeGrasse Tyson say on a talk show that 400,000 people are murdered every year around the world. That's closing in on half a million murders a year by people. Why would murder come so naturally to supposedly civilized, sophisticated, pious people? It is because we are taught that killing is the natural order of things, ordained by an all-good, all-powerful god or inviolable evolution. So, psycho god supposedly gave us dominion over all the other animals, and we took it to the sickest extremes of torture, enslavement, and murder. Because, what would psycho god do? He who ostensibly created a system of obligate murder to survive?

As long as religions keep offering this violent, angry, jealous, demanding, very male god as perfect, good, loving and omnipotent, violence is justifiable and inevitable. God does it, so it must be OK, so long as it's for the right cause (and everyone is sure their cause is the right cause). This god was created by primitive men in their own image. Primitive men were the ones who wanted to use killing and physical force to keep control over women, other tribes and the other animals.

Dominion is the excuse religionists and even most carnivorous non-religionists assert for our horrible behavior toward other animals, but what's the difference between humans and the other animals that somehow makes us superior or justifiably dominant? Language? That human capacity is, as yet, not fully understood. We don't yet know for certain why we have our specific language ability and other animals don't. It may just be a physical, evolutionary adaptation. There are lots of theories, and most are extremely anthropocentric. And we know that the other animals have communication systems, just not language in the human sense.

Language is a super important skill, but I don't think it makes humans superior to other animals. If it did, then people who had superior language skills would be superior to other people who do not. Do we accept that as true? No, we accept it as different people having different abilities. There are some humans who will never be able to think and speak in a sophisticated manner. Should they be enslaved or eaten? This would be very bad news for the trump cult members, who can literally not use language to process information and assert reasonable conclusions. They're acting on 100% adrenaline (the fear hormone) produced by the most primitive, reptilian part of the brain, and 0% language and meaning processing, which is produced by the more advanced, supposedly human part of the brain. Watch some Jordan Klepper clips of brief interviews with trump cult members for confirmation of this.

This whole concept of dominion that we use to justify our horrific treatment of animals based on our supposed superiority, generalizes to our treatment of each other. If humans have different levels of functioning, and they definitely do, then the same reasoning we apply to why we have dominion over animals allows us to claim dominion over lower functioning people, people who don't communicate well or do well in academics or even dance and sing well. I wonder how we'd feel about a system that allowed Phds to eat high school drop outs, rock stars to eat their audience members, and athletes to eat anyone they could catch and subdue. It also is used by racists and chauvinists to erroneously claim the inferiority of other groups, thus justifying enslaving them and committing genocide against them. Newsflash: god has always been used as evidence of others' inferiority, to claim they are uncivilized, heathen savages and thus not quite worthy of being treated as equals. Hmm, sounds exactly like the food chain argument we use to eat animals.

A vast majority of the human population live in situations that play out a wholly human version of the predator–prey paradigm, from nations living under kleptocracies to nearly entire continents living under insane, genocidal warlords. Even democracies are so fragile that a two hundred year old noble experiment is regressing to a racist kakistocracy (rule by the worst) due to the greed and insecurity of its citizens. (Yes, I'm talking to you, trumpster trash.)

The beautiful Russian culture didn't even last as a democracy for two decades before some beady eyed, little troll of a psychopath wrested it away from them. They were finally happy and prosperous, free to express their creativity, and now they're back to harsh repressions, and millions of good Russians have had to become virtually stateless to avoid the predator putin, and those were the lucky ones who had the resources to escape. Not to mention the unforgiveable atrocities he is committing against the Ukrainians. Is putin even human? Are psychopaths human? Can one be human without a conscience? Even the supposedly "lower" animals have consciences. But psychopaths like trump and putin don't. Maybe human and humanoid are two different concepts. I would argue that you have to have a conscience to be fully human.

All this brings into question the nature of a supposed god who loves his creation and wants what's best for it, but sure doesn't show it. Which in turn, brings us back to that classic theological paradox, the "Problem of Evil". If god is all good, then he would not allow evil to exist, so he must not be all powerful to prevent it. If he were all powerful and allowed evil to exist, then he couldn't be all good. Religious apologists have been grappling with this conundrum for millennia and they have been unable to resolve it. They have attempted to fabricate the most convoluted and complex of solutions, but they cannot succeed. The most well known and accepted excuse as I mentioned, is that good old, reliable, stale inanity, the "inscrutability defense". God is so superior to us that we cannot understand the great mind of god and should not even try, steering us handily back to obedience and faith, which religionists try to pass off as an innate good.

Faith is not however, intrinsically positive. Having faith in the wrong things can be very harmful indeed. It's a good girl falling for a bad boy. It's a cult member believing in a sociopath leader. It's an abused spouse staying with her abuser. Faith in the wrong things or persons destroys lives.

The inscrutability defense is problematic in so many ways, but here's one I want to expand on a bit. Remember that all wrong-doers believe they have some justification for their actions. They could just plead inscrutability as their defense. They could claim that society simply isn't sophisticated enough to understand their very appropriate motives, just like god. And when the prosecutor responded to the defendant, "Well, you aren't god," he could just say, "How do you know? Prove that I'm not. Oh, right, you can't prove a negative." When I worked in the Criminal Justice system as a Criminal *Defense* Investigator, I knew of a rape defendant who claimed that forcing sex on his victim was just his way of proposing to her. See, his motives were just inscrutable. He was just misunderstood. Fortunately, this inscrutability defense didn't work out for him. Trumpster trash are actually claiming something of the sort for hitler now. Putin thinks his actions are justified but inscrutable to the west. Inscrutability is the slipperiest of slopes.

Theologians having failed to reconcile the "Problem of Evil" for millennia, we are left with the question of why god would not only allow evil, but as has been shown, ostensibly create evil. But I am going to give you an answer right here, right now. And, like I said, you aren't going to like it.

The only possible resolution to how god can be all good and all powerful but still allow evil is that there must be a reason for the evil, which in turn results in ultimate good. It is a lesson, a puzzle inserted into the creation as a test for us and our big, sophisticated brains. We must solve the puzzle, eliminating the evil that he provided as a test problem, in order to pass the test. Otherwise, either god created an unintelligent design, or he is so evil he likes all the suffering, and he is basically Satan. ***We are charged with eradicating violence, hatred and suffering even though the entire "creation"*** *is based on those very things.* That is our test and our purpose, if you truly believe in god (and frankly, even if you don't, and believe alternatively in evolution). There is no other possible intelligent solution to the "Problem of Evil" without resorting to the impotent inscrutability defense. We are supposed to rectify the food chain and all the evil violence it has wrought, essentially fix god's mistake. We must evolve enough to accomplish this task in order to save ourselves.

And we have failed abysmally.

There was even a ***HUGE*** hint in the Old Testament:

Isaiah 11:6-8 – "The wolf shall dwell with the lamb, and the leopard shall lie down with the kid, and the calf and the lion and the fatling together, and a child shall lead them. The cow and the bear shall feed; their young shall lie down together; and the lion shall eat

straw like the ox." It was such an important clue that they even repeated it in Isaiah 65:25 – "The wolf and the lamb shall feed together, the lion shall eat straw like the ox; and dust shall be the serpent's food. They shall not hurt or destroy in all my holy mountain, says the lord."

If you truly believe the Bible is god's word, then that passage tells you god's vision for paradise on Earth. Not working toward making it a reality is disobeying your god.

But who the fuck does god think he is, giving us a little test?! Why didn't he just create a peaceful, perfect paradise for us in the first place without all the petty commandments about obedience? If he truly loved us, he could have made us perfect, we wouldn't need a test to make us evolve, and we could just all be happy. So, really does petty god really exist? If so, why? He seems to serve no purpose but his own ego. God is just that abusive father who beats you to a pulp every day and then forces you to say you love him in order to get a little dinner, that abusive husband who insults you in public and then wants to fuck when you get home. Just a sociopathic creep, and the amalgamation of all the worst human traits.

Instead of correcting the food chain, we exalt it just as it is. Clearly to remedy god's food chain error, we must stop it, starting with us. Your god requires us to all become vegans immediately (and so does evolution of our big brains, by the way). This is the only possible action if you want to believe in an all-good, all-powerful god-- to correct the test error he inserted into his creation in order to teach us something. Otherwise your god is just a ridiculous paradox that you cling to like a scared child to an insane parent. If you continue to eat the other animals of the planet, you are an Atheist. Or worse, you are a Satanist, worshipping an evil god.

Now, you will protest that this doesn't undo the evil food chain, it only breaks one link of it. The other predators will continue to wreak mayhem. And you're partly right. Not only must humans quit killing to live, but we must also give every other living being on Earth the means and will to be able to live without killing. Yes, even lions and crocodiles.

That's impossible! you will protest. It's an absurd endeavor! This from the species who figured out how to fly, how to breathe under water, how to use fire and wheels, and build skyscrapers, cathedrals and suspension bridges to name but a few. Not to mention, the species who revels in bending nature to its will. But we can't resolve how to properly nourish "obligate" carnivores without violence? Puh—leeeze!

Actually, we are already part way there. I became a vegetarian in 1977. Veggie burgers tasted like sawdust and there was no such thing as a cheese substitute, let alone one that didn't taste like plastic. I almost starved to death. I didn't know how to cook and I didn't even like fruit and veggies. But I had picked up a package of rib-eye steak at the supermarket and suddenly realized that the euphemistically-called "juice" on the package that was getting on my hands was blood. So, that settled that. I dropped that bloody thing like a hot potato, and I stopped eating meat.

Since then, many wonderful companies and individuals have intelligently created tasty vegan foods that are delicious, despite the stale comedic trope that vegan food is boring, inedible, and a fate worse than death. (Get with the times and do some research, Comedians, or risk telling stale jokes.) And that's just what they're producing for us who are not interested in the taste of meat anymore. In addition, they have developed beet-juice-dripping meat substitutes that actually taste like beef. I know, because I accidentally ate some and it was so like meat that I was grossed out by it. This is how we'll get the lions and other predators. It will work, because we'll figure out how to do it, just like we've figured out how to erect domes, arches and flying buttresses.

OK, anticipating your next argument (because I've heard them all a million times): "But what about plants? They're living things and you're killing them to make all these plant-based meat substitutes," you complain. Right. Plants don't generally consume other living beings to survive (except those insectivorous venus fly traps, the little fuckers). Dear, sweet, gentle plants live innocuous lives of quiet photosynthesis, gathering their life force from sunshine. Their worst infraction is crowding each other out and falling on each other in death. They do not deserve to be the world's dinner any more than sweet bunnies.

But, you know, you don't have to kill most plants to eat what you need. Soy beans, which form the basis of many meat substitutes, and beans, nuts, fruits and some vegetables can be harvested without killing the whole plant. If we didn't insist on having eight fucking BILLION humans on the planet, we could harvest what we need gently, respectfully, and sustainably. (Remember, we made the David and the Sistine chapel, so we have the creativity and sensitivity to do this. It's just a matter of making it a priority.)

When you pick a home grown tomato you don't have to yank it violently from its stalk, you can just gently pry it away at the optimal time. The plant will probably feel like, "Thank god that big oaf is off there. She was dragging me down." Grains are harvested after the plant has died in the case of wheat, or some such as rice can be gently harvested without killing the plant. I believe root vegetables can be harvested after the supporting plant has died. Also, while they have the same survival instinct as all living things and should definitely be respected, plants don't have nerve endings to cause them pain, like animals do, although, some studies suggest plants exhibit a stress reaction to violence, thus the need for respect, gentleness, and non-lethal harvesting.

So, my objections to the unintelligent design that is the food chain, so far, are cruelty, competition, and horror, (not to mention the environmental impact and inefficiency, which is discussed at great length and to the point of proof by other authors in other essays). These conditions create a negative environment for the sociological and psychological development of individuals and societies. Survival trumps the tendency toward self actualization, as explained by Maslow. In the food chain system that we accept as natural (and even desirable since it was supposedly bestowed by a benevolent benefactor or nature), the competition that is constantly required for survival stunts creativity, altruism, and enjoyment of life.

To summarize, this worst idea that mankind has ever invented, god, whose ostensible design for us is the absolute worst, holds us back from realizing our full potential. "He" is a convenient excuse for the greedy because they can claim that winners and the consequent losers are the natural order of things ordained by an all-knowing, all-good god, so if you're a loser, you're just not trying hard enough and if they're the winners, it's not because they inherited it from their ruthless daddy, it's that they deserve it. Instead of forming societies where achievers are motivated by a desire to bring everyone along with their progress, we have formed a system whereby individuals are encouraged to compete for and hoard resources to the detriment of others. And the all-knowing, all-good god made it that way, so it's OK.

Now, I have to mention that there is another answer, besides inscrutability that religious nuts come up with to the Problem of Evil, and I'd be remiss if I didn't dispose of it with the dismissive disdain it deserves. They will claim that there's evil because god gave humans free will. Yes, evil is all our fault! OK. How would that explain environmentally caused famine, disaster, disease, even unrequited love? And why do bad things happen to good people if free will explains evil? How is a rescue worker who is killed by a falling building in an aftershock while helping a quake victim explained by anyone's free will? You have to resort to god's inscrutability, so that's the end of free will.

The only place to go from there, and religious nuts **will** go there, is to blame the victim for their own plight- got cancer due to lifestyle (really ?everyone? there'd be no cancer if people lived right?) got murdered because you hung with the wrong people or went to the wrong place, got raped because you dressed too provocatively, you're starving because you don't pick yourself up by your boot straps, you lost your home in a tornado because you lived in the wrong place, you suffered unrequited love because you're not holy enough… etc, etc, etc, ad nauseam. They are mean people. Not to mention ignorant.

It's astonishing how religionists give god credit for all the good in the world, but blame humanity or themselves for all the bad. How are they any different from an abused spouse who finds some reason to blame herself for the beating administered by her violent wreck of a husband? Dinner was late, so… C'mon!

Once you've disposed of inscrutability and free will, there is no place left to turn for the devout but faith and punishment. It always comes back to faith and fear, and just a reminder, faith is not always positive, although people thoughtlessly proclaim it so.

For Atheists, it always comes back to evolution. Humans love to claim that our fellow primates, our immediate evolutionary antecedents, are natural omnivores, so it follows that humans evolved as omnivores, but that may be stretching the truth to defend humans' carnivorism. Primate diets consist mostly of leaves, fruits, flowers and seeds, with *some* primates making very *occasional* forays into meat eating. We have all seen primates at the zoo enjoying grasses and other plant material at feeding time. We never see the attendant throw a hunk of meat into the primate enclosure. So, it's not at all natural for humans to eat meat, especially in the quantities we consume. We just greedily, competitively decided to. Then we invented a supernatural overlord who gave us permission. Why do you need to invent permission if you don't think you're doing anything wrong?

Are primates even competitive, as opposed to cooperative? Or is that just humans observing through an anthropocentric lens? An occasional skirmish does not a competitive society make. Ants and bees are wired for cooperation, not competition (and I didn't claim they were democratic, that's a whole different issue). So, it is possible for animals to be naturally cooperative. Maybe more animals are cooperative than we perceive through our competitive, biased human filter.

So, how did we humans get to be this blood-thirsty and competitive? *It was not inevitable.* Somewhere along the way we made the choice, and therefore, we can change it.

Chapter 2- Way Smarter than God

You might be thinking, "If she's so against the food chain and thinks god did such a lousy job, does she think she could come up with something better?" Oh, yeah, I know I can. Basically, anyone who gave it some thought could do better than god has supposedly done.

Were I your benevolent, omnipotent creator, I would have designed a planet where all the leaves that were shed by trees each year would be the tastiest, most nutritious of substances from which we could make all manner and variety of delicious dishes. They could be ground up into various types of flours, each with their own distinct taste. Same with whatever animals shed- tasty, omnipresent and variable. Nothing from living things would go to waste. (Why would a smart, kind God build waste into a finite system?) All we'd have to do is gather these culinary delights and process them into food. And we, who engineered the pyramids and the internet could do that with our eyes closed and our hands tied behind our backs, all without harming a single living being. Between that and the fruits and veggies we would gently, respectfully harvest, we'd be living in an epicurean paradise.

But we would have to make sure that there was always the right amount for the number of living beings that needed sustenance. This would entail maintaining proper population. So, instead of installing unlimited sperm and eggs in animals, each would have a set supply that may or may not be used during their lifetime. Once a male fertilized two eggs, his body would quit making reproductive sperm. Likewise, once a female had had two eggs fertilized, her body would quit producing eggs. Nobody could have more than two offspring. Life would be less of a drudgery without all those young to raise, and people would be happier and less stressed.

Also, if you knew you could have only two babies, you might be a lot more careful about what, I mean who, you reproduced with. I'm talking to you, women who are desperate to reproduce because society tells you, you must, and then you end up accidentally reproducing with some sociopath, and end up raising a little junior sociopath, one of the most unpleasant of life experiences. But more on sociopaths and how to avoid them later. Pay attention when we get there, because this is VERY important information.

In my creation, people would live to be 75-80. There would be no disease, no accidental death, certainly no murder and life would end at an age when you'd had enough and could look forward to eternal rest after a long, but finite productive life of your choosing. In my little paradisical creation of 75 guaranteed years, the greatest sorrow would be unrequited love, but we could learn to deal with that, because without having to scrape for our basic needs, we would have the capacity to self actualize enough to realize that romantic rejection shouldn't be taken personally- it's simply a matter of incompatibility.

Mammals wouldn't have those pesky hormones that make us gravitate to those brawny but assholic males. We would actually gravitate to the more loving supportive, FEMINIST males. And males wouldn't be full of that toxic testosterone that makes them the assholes they are. Mammals would all be attractive, but in different ways. Nobody would be homely or ugly or whiney, and selecting a partner would be more like going to a bakery and selecting what appeals to you, out of an array of attractive options. Why the hell did god make people ugly or smelly or stupid? How cruel. Why couldn't everybody be attractive in their own way and then you had to find the one most compatible with you? If god had made everyone attractive, Madge Taylor Greene and Matt Gaetz wouldn't be such whiney, insecure assholes. They might be normal, because they wouldn't have to compensate for their inferiority by trying to place others beneath them.

Since I'm the creator, I can do whatever I want and everything I created would be nice. There would be no ugly smells. Why should feces smell bad? Why shouldn't it just smell like baked goods, or whatever yummy concoction you ate previously? Why can't digestive stomach acid smell like flowers? God didn't have to make body odors and people with stinky feet. He didn't have to make bad breath or farts. It almost seems as though he was a 14 year old boy who liked bathroom humor. These things, like the food chain, prove that there is no intelligent design, just random biological evolution. A benevolent creator simply would not have added these nuisances, unless it's all for the benefit of lazier comedians (you know, the same ones who joke about vegan food).

And what the hell is the deal with hymens???!!!! What the fuck is even the evolutionary function of that little pain in the vagina? Men seem to think they serve the same purpose as those tissue sashes hotels put around toilet seats that read, "Sanitized for your protection". If anything needs a "Sanitized for your protection" sign, it's dicks! Men are such whores, they'll stick those things in anywhere! Men should have to put a little "Sanitized for your protection" tissue sleeve on their dicks every time they take a shower, so a woman knows it's safe to use. (Of course, I have already mentioned there will be no disease in my creation, so VD's not an issue.) Finally, a species' penises should be no larger than the species' vaginas- just a nice, snug fit with no stretching. Why wouldn't an intelligent, benevolent god have done that?

And childbirth! WTF!!!???? Babies should be fully formed and ready for live birth when they're no bigger than the size of the species' penis, which will have to all be the same size within a species in order to avoid racism and insecurity. These little penis-sized babies would just gush right out like they were on a water slide. They'd be giggling and happy when they were born and their mother wouldn't be an exhausted, haggard wreck. Dads would love it because they could begin playing with their kids right at birth by catching them, which is all dads want to do with their children anyway. (Of course, women would have a reliable girlfriend there for back up, just in case.) Hell, it's all any of us want to do with babies and kids, is play with them and enjoy them, truth be told, but then kids just turn out to need so much care, work and maintenance. Constant maintenance! That's when the unintended drudgery kicks in and it's all downhill from there. You have to intricately plan date nights and find a babysitter, then the dad drives the sitter home and…

And OMG, the "creator" is so incompetent that he put the clitoris in the wrong place!!!!! Clits should be right inside the vagina, where they can benefit from all the activity going on in there, not miss half of it due to the incompetence and selfishness of men! God couldn't even find the g-spot, like most men! Instead, god put it right outside the vagina , so that it's literally easier to masturbate! (Half the men reading this are thinking, "Oh, so *that's* where it is!) Wait! Maybe it's one of those puzzles that god likes to make us solve, like the Problem of Evil, so men if you can't bring on the orgasms every time, YOU an Atheist!!!! But wait, wait, wait! Placement of the clit by god is much better suited for oral sex than intercourse, so apparently god has ordained that men should be giving women constant oral sex. So, if you're not performing cunnilingus all the time, YOU an Atheist! (And Atheists should do it for the same reason women give you bj's, because they love you and want to make you feel good.)

So, another riddle solved. God put the clit where it is to make men either get the job done during intercourse, or be prepared to stay awake and attentive until you complete the task with oral sex. Oh, does that sound like too much trouble? Then now you know how she feels after working all day, coming home and doing most or all of the family work, and then you want her to hump your dead ass when there's probably nothing in it for her? You're a monster! Now, get down there and finish the job! And if you don't know how, then ask! Figure it out. Show some initiative.

Upshot, if you have intercourse and you come before she does, then you are expected to finish the job competently. You don't get to wear her down with your incompetence until she gives up and tells you to just forget it. If you're too tired, oh, boo hoo hoo the fuck hoo! Finish the job. You don't get to go home from work after lunch just because you need a nap. You'd get fired if you did. Finish the damn job!

Waaah! You cry. Women are so much more difficult to climax than men. It's too harrrrrd! Then maybe god made it that way to punish men for being lazy, and not doing their share, but you've still got to do it.

What do the food chain and the clit have in common? They are both test errors in creation (or evolution) that humans are meant to correct, utilizing our big, evolved brains- that's what they're for, not for thinking up ways to cheat and steal from each other!

Hymens, childbirth, and clits definitely add to the evidence that there is no god and there is no intelligent design. But of course, primitive men used these phenomena as proof that their nasty god had cursed women for being bad and, you know, wanting to eat from the tree of (god forbid) **_knowledge_**!

And frankly, speaking of dick size, that argues against a benevolent god, too. Like bad odors and other embarrassments, why would an all-good god make men have different size penises? It makes them so insecure and jealous of each other. And it makes them racist because of that insecurity. It makes them violent, it makes them drive big gas guzzlers and pick-up trucks even though they have no cargo to pick up, it makes them augment their tiny penises with long, dangerous, lead shooting phalluses (you know, guns), and it causes all manner of other bad behaviors in men. I'm talking to you, putin and trump. And bolsinaro, netanyahu, orban, dutarte, xi, mbs, milei, and too many more to mention. Tiny penises, every one!

When I was in college, I dated a black man who was an absolute asshole. One day, he explained to me that the reason white men were so rabidly racist was because they knew black men had bigger dicks than them. At the time, I dismissed this as the self-serving social hypothesis of a chauvinist jerk and rolled my eyes at him. As time went on, I learned it was the one thing he had gotten right. White men, the more racist you are, the smaller your penis is. It's a fact. And you're giving yourselves away, I'm sorry. Now everyone knows. You've been pantsed and everyone knows you're racist because you have a tiny penis. Maybe quit being racist and you can pull up your pants and have some dignity. Also, the gas guzzler and the gun worship give it away. No one cares about the size of your dick but you- get over yourselves!

Design, especially "Intelligent Design" insinuates that there was a purpose behind the project. Art is produced to be beautiful or make a statement. Clothing is designed to adorn humans. Well, Earth seems to me to be the prison jumpsuit of design, very basic. It doesn't seem like a lot of thought was put into it. It's just barely functional, as designs go. If the Earth had been designed, not just spun randomly in some fashion from matter in the universe, it should be more hospitable to its life forms. But again, that's what our big, evolved brains are for. We are supposed to take this prison shift of a world and turn it into haute couture- not an impossible task, but it's going to take a lot of creativity. There may be a lot of toilet paper carnations involved.

Here's a thought. Why didn't the creator design Earth with concentric islands ringing the planet latitudinally from the equator to the poles? It could have beaches on all sides of each island with mountains, lakes, springs, deserts, prairies and savannahs in the interiors of the islands. That way, there would be plenty of beachfront property for everyone who wanted it, but also other landscapes for those preferring them. Those who liked seasons could live in latitudes closer to the poles, but those who favor year round summer could live closer to the equator. Why didn't our loving creator make that for us? Because plate tectonics made the landscapes, not a designer, that's why.

Also, and this is a good one, why didn't the creator think to make cum taste like chocolate and be chock full of nutrients? I guarantee you, there would not be 8 fucking BILLION humans on the planet if cum tasted like chocolate. Intercourse would be for intentional procreation only, because no animal would want to waste all that chocolatey goodness on their genitals which have virtually no taste buds. Also, men would finish the job, every time, with no whining!!!! (Of course, men would complain that cum should taste like beer, but we are not having that yeasty smell in our vaginas, so just forget that and refine your taste buds to appreciate chocolate!) The other animals could smugly disdain us for our inferiority in flexibility, being unable to lick ourselves and partake of chocolate whenever we wanted. (Every yoga teacher would be a millionaire.)

I'm just sayin'. I definitely could have done a better job designing a world than god has done, and I bet you could too. What interesting design flourishes would you come up with?

Chapter 3- Smarter than god and a bigger dick, too- A Brief History of the Invention of god

So, now we're going to get into the brief history of the invention of god. This pertains to the Abrahamic god of Judaism, Christianity and Islam, but it probably explains the invention of all gods. Gods in general, and Abraham's god in particular were invented by primitive men (and I don't mean people, I mean male humans) for fear control and especially power consolidation. Gods are not revealed in magic books and through mystic revelations, but are purposefully created to achieve specific political objectives.

The Abrahamic god was invented because the early Hebrews lived in a desirable location of fertile land beside a teeming sea. They had perfect soil for growing olive trees and olive oil was their big resource, like putin's fucking oil. Because of the ugly system of competition and scarce resources, i.e. god's moronic food chain, other people wanted the Hebrews' land and stuff. They were always being invaded by empires to their north and south, and by tribes from the east, and eventually from the sea to the west.

The poor, put-upon, hapless Hebrews lived in constant fear of extinction. Yahweh (the name of the Abrahamic god) was invented to assuage the peoples' fear of the violent attackers. A powerful god would protect them, because they were his people. So, Yahweh must be a stern, mean, vengeful god who seemed ultra fearsome. He must be willing to smite, vanquish and do violence to protect the Hebrews. In short, they needed a strong, unrestrained psychopath to protect them, so that's exactly what they invented. They didn't even come up with this idea first. They kind of copied from the other tribes' gods, Baal, Ashteroth, etc. It was in vogue to have an insanely violent, vengeful, psychopathic god back then and the Hebrews had to be able to compete. There are at least four or five other regional gods mentioned in the Bible. It takes the entire Pentateuch (first five books of the Old Testament) to arrive at Yahweh as the most powerful god, let alone the only god. So, when the Hebrews were having troubles, they would brag to their tormenters that their powerful, vengeful god Yahweh would smite them. My god's bigger than your god, an early version of the big dick contest.

The Hebrews were invaded and ultimately conquered by five empires in succession over a few centuries: Assyria, Babylon, Persia, Macedonia (Greece under Alexander the Great) and Rome. This seems like that really boring ancient history they skimmed over in high school World History class, because even your teacher thought it was a major yawn-fest. But it's actually quite relevant to us today. When Assyria conquered the northern Hebrew nation, Israel, this led to the emergence of the southern Hebrew nation, Judea, as the more important of the two states. That's why Jews are called Jews and not usually Hebrews or Israelites, although all can be used. There are a lot of confusing, conflicting stories in the Torah or Old Testament, because some of it was written by the northern Israelites and some was written by the southern Judeans.

But to get on with it, after the Assyrians rent the Hebrew nation in two by conquering the wealthier northern Hebrew land of Israel, the poor, country cousins to the south in Judea gained ascendancy, and rewrote a lot of history to glorify their group. The story of Judean David, the great but unconfirmable king was introduced to Hebrew lore as well as the legend of the first temple in Judean Jerusalem. No archaeological evidence of the first temple or David has ever been found, and believe me when I tell you, they've tried, thus my calling it a legend. This was a case of country bumpkin cousins making up tales to elevate their status, like you might intentionally falsely claim to have a celebrity ancestor to impress your competitors and enhance your credentials.

After the Assyrians, the Babylonians came along and conquered the Hebrews again, this time employing the age-old, nation-destroying technique of exiling all the leaders to Babylon. But then, a few generations later, the Persian king Cyrus conquered the Hebrews and the Babylonians and made the Babylonians send all the exiled Hebrew leaders home to Palestine, even though they had lived their whole lives in Babylon. Not to be discouraged, when the alien Hebrew leaders returned to Palestine, they just reclaimed leadership of the Hebrews and started bossing them around, making them stand around and listen to endless recitations of the returned exiles' revised scriptures, made them divorce their non-Jewish wives and generally made nuisances of themselves by wreaking havoc on the ordinary folks' lives. In short, they were religious nuts imposing their will on people who had until then enjoyed a more easy-going lifestyle. So, this overbearing religious nuttery has been going on for millennia. Madge Taylor Greene's ilk are as old as time.

Eventually, along came Alexander the Great and he claimed Israel (Palestine) for Macedonia and the rules began to relax under this Greek influence, which caused the conservative Jews to go nuts, thinking the conquerors were being too lax and allowing the Jews to enjoy life too much, like god forbid, attending public nude baths and calisthenics. So that caused intra-tribal conflict, because the conservative Jews thought the liberal Jews were grooming pious, young Jewish men for god knows what! (Sounds familiar- some things never change.) This is the time of the Maccabees, ostensible Jewish heroes who fought the Greek reformers and their Jewish supporters, "resanctified" a supposedly-defiled temple and invented the "miracle" of the one day supply of oil lasting eight days (the origin story of Chanukah).

Finally Romans conquered Palestine and the pious, conservative Jews became so troublesome, in the end, the Romans began to actually outlaw some Jewish traditions and practices in an attempt to mainstream this annoying little backwater province into the greater Roman empire. Which, of course, made the conservative Jews go nuts.

Mind you, many proud Jews liked the new, more liberal rules and practices, but due to the agitation, assassinations and general guerilla tactics of the conservatives against the Romans, the Jews were suppressed by the Romans and their unique identity became threatened. It's always the fundamentalists screwing everything up for everybody. The empires didn't give a damn about that Palestinian hinterland as long as it just paid its taxes and didn't cause any trouble, but nooooo… the crazy fundamentalists just couldn't go along with the program and conduct their weird religious practices in private where no one would care what they did, and they pissed off the subjugating overlords so much, they got everybody into hot water to where their identity was vengefully threatened with extinction.

And that is why these five empires who defeated the Hebrews of Palestine in succession over a few centuries are so important. They caused the Hebrews to feel constantly under threat, with their freedoms and rights randomly being granted, then curtailed. Out of this persistent paranoia and vulnerability grew the messiah idea, a savior to preserve their unique identity and community. By the time of the Roman conquest the idea that a human messiah was coming to lead the Hebrews to victory was part of mainstream Jewish tradition. And out of that prevalent belief, well, the rest is history- Jesus was nominated by some rag tag disciples as the Jewish messiah and through a series of odd historical flukes, against all odds, it stuck. (There were other messianic claimants who did not stick, e.g. the leader in the Dead Sea Scrolls.)

The odd occurrences that caused the astonishing random ascendancy of Christianity include the conversion of Saul/Paul, an enterprising fellow with somewhat influential contacts among the Roman overlords, deciding Jesus was a good economic hook. He was a great promoter, a guy who knew how to get things done, and he started the small cult of Jesus after Jesus' death. Paul knew how to start a lucrative, new religion and he really knew how to sell it, door to door, town to town, and epistle to epistle. Then, the promise of eternal life angle, and the pogroms against the Christian Jews which demonstrated they were willing to die for their beliefs impressed The Gullible into thinking there might be something to this Jesus cult.

There was a brief but intense schism early on over whether converted Gentiles had to comply with mandatory circumcision, for obvious reasons (men and their strong feelings about their precious penises), but this was overcome with the anti-dick-snipping faction winning the day (hey, tithes are tithes, wherever they come from).

The really big, decisive milestone came about three centuries later when Roman Emperor Constantine's mother joined the cult and convinced her son to adopt Christianity as the state religion, an advantageous move for the cunning ruler who sought to assimilate the small-but-growing, troublesome cult and use it as his own power base consolidating both religious and political power in himself. And appeasing his Mom in the process. Win, win!

So, again, who cares about this ancient history? Well, we all should because it is the fundamental basis of western society much the same as the food chain is the fundamental basis of life on Earth. All our morals, laws, practices, customs, behaviors, in short our entire western culture has been affected by the small, justifiably paranoid nation of Hebrews who invented a messiah to assuage their fears, which in turn by happenstance turned into the worldwide religion and power base of Christianity, which affects every single aspect of our lives today. If Assyria, Babylon, Persia, Macedonia and Rome had just minded their own business and kept their greedy mitts off the Hebrews' olive oil and land, we would probably be living in a very different society today. Perhaps one that was free of religious weirdoes, because maybe our entire society wouldn't be based on a philosophy that arose from paranoia and fear. I'm just saying… It could have gone a different way, a better way.

Isn't it ironic that one of the first things we used our evolutionarily advanced, big brains for was to invent the fraudulent, unsophisticated security system that is religion, in order to allay our most primitive instinct- fear. And then the system requires the suspension of our sophisticated brains in order to believe it. The circle of stupidity.

But humans are stupid, filthy animals and they grasp at any old straw for security. And you know what Ben Franklin said, "A society who forfeits freedom for security deserves neither". And that's exactly what Judeo-Christian-Islamic society gives us- neither.

There is a very amusing story in the Old Testament or the Torah about an arrogant conqueror boasting that he has defeated all the other tribes and he names their gods one by one stating that they could not help their people, so what makes the Hebrews think their Yahweh will be able to defeat him? (2 Kings 18-35). You'd think the outcome of this story would be that Yahweh helped his people overcome the overly confident invader, wouldn't you? But you'd be wrong. I've always thought this story was left in the Bible by accident. The general defeats the Hebrews and they have to pay tribute to him for decades (which fact is whitewashed in the biblical version). Oops! Was Yahweh busy the day of the invasion? Absent-minded, psychopath god. There's never a cop around when you need one.

Another Bible story recounts the tale of the Hebrews themselves defeating another tribe, and Yahweh orders the victors to leave no one alive (a real mensch of a god), to slaughter every woman, child and man of the opposing tribe, in short, to commit genocide, but the Hebrew conquerors show "mercy" and slaughter only the men (I guess wanting to keep the women and children for rape and slavery). Yahweh gets pissed because his orders were disobeyed and he exacts a terrible revenge and curses them forever. He sounds nice, insisting on genocide.

God was always about power and never about love or good behavior. The correct behavior part came along so that men could exert power over women and lower status men, under threat of provoking god. Powerful men would tell you how to act to avoid the wrath of god, and thus keep you beholden to them through all manner of injustice inflicted upon you. Oddly, that's been working on The Gullible for over 5,000 years.

How do I know this history of the invention of god? I was curious as to why people ostensibly believed such an utterly far-fetched religious bill of goods, so I did a lot of reading of popular texts extracted from scholarly research (rather than wade through the brain-numbing, jargon-infested, snooze-fest academic books and journals in the field). Please see the bibliography at the end for details and further reading, and forgive that it was so long ago (like, two decades) that I read these fine books, that I can no longer parse the appropriate citations. If any author feels their ideas should be credited, please let me know, and I'll confirm it and do so. I don't mean to steal people's original ideas. In fact, I'd be horrified. Perhaps scholars will be relieved not to be cited in this work. It is pretty undignified and unscholarly, what with all the outrageous profanity and blasphemy.

I never did quite find out why humans still believe this nonsense. Many posit that it's ingrained, genetically programmed into our species, but I don't buy that. More on that later.

My conclusion: They don't really believe it. They can't. For the same reason a child can't sustain belief in Santa Claus beyond the age of 9, adult humans can't really believe in god. When a child begins to question Santa, they ask such questions as, "How does he make it around the whole world in one night and stop at every house? How does he carry that many toys? Why do some kids from the poor neighborhood get so fewer presents than other kids?" You can answer with "magic" to the first two queries, but how are you going to explain away the third?

The same problem with god. How does that guy in the sky keep track of all eight fucking billion of us? How does he hear all the prayers? Magic. Faith. But why are some most urgent of prayers not answered, like a young mother surviving cancer, while other dumb prayers like winning the state championship are? Yeah, I know he's too inscrutable for the lowly likes of me to understand and he never gives you more than you can handle and blah, blah, blah. It's the same comforting pabulum we feed children about Santa Claus. Until it just can't convince them anymore. (It also helps that other kids will eventually laugh at them and call them babies, if they believe. Is that what we need to do to religionists? Laugh at them? We're trying, but they just get mad and threaten to shoot us.) God's supposed inscrutability isn't much of a comfort nor an acceptable answer when you lose something vital, like your loved one or your health.

When kids get too sophisticated to truly believe in Santa anymore two things begin to occur: They start asking questions and they get mad at the truth. No one defends the existence of Santa Claus more vehemently than a questioning nine year old. My nine-year-old niece asked me if Santa Claus was real because she knew I'd tell her the truth. She was hoping I'd confirm he was real, and when I told her the truth, she got so mad, like it was my fault there is no Santa Claus. Like all the religious nuts will get mad at me for telling them there is no god.

That's where humanity is with Santa god. We *are* too sophisticated and educated, and we know too much and have too much ability to reason, to believe in Santa god. But people don't want to give up this happy bonanza of possibly granted wishes. So like angry, petulant children, they become gundamentalists and double down on their ostensible belief in god. They get really angry at anyone who doesn't believe in their imaginary friend. They even blame the non-believers for all the troubles of the world because the non-believers are pissing god off and ruining it for the rest of humanity, like their accusation that Gays in New Orleans caused Hurricane Katrina. Despite no evidence for the existence of god and despite much evidence against it, they desperately want to believe in their Santa god. Why?

1) Some want to believe in god because they think that it makes them a good person. All Atheists are evil murderers and all Christians are model citizens, they think. This is why I was a Christian as a teenager. I thought it made me a good person, a rudimentary conclusion appropriate for a child but not an adult, who has many experiences to the contrary. Being religious in no way makes one a good person. Some of the finest people are Atheists and some of the worst people are devoutly religious.

2) Many people turn to religion in times of rehabilitation, be it for crime, addiction, grief, depression or whatever, and they then ascribe their recovery to god. God made them a better person to overcome their issues because they prayed to him, they believe. But this is just an error. God didn't rehabilitate them, they did it themselves. They worked their butts off to transcend a terrible problem and then gave the credit to an imaginary friend. This unfortunately diminishes their accomplishment and weakens their newfound fortification. God does not make you good or happy or strong. You do. But that is one of the reasons people

cling so desperately to belief in god, because they believe it makes them good and strong.

3) Another reason people convince themselves to believe is that religions provide community and social networks. Folks may enjoy the social atmosphere at church, talking with others, singing, handling snakes together(?), talking in magical, exclusive tongues (?), or just the very normal feeling of having a close knit group of friends to get together with. A friend of mine changed denominations three times in the course of less than a decade and he never cited the new church as having better nuanced religious principles, but instead spoke of more welcoming congregants or better music. He spent one of his two precious days off from work per week at church because of the sense of community he derived from it. Which is fine to aspire to community, but the same could be achieved with a book club where you didn't have to believe the book was magical.

4) Some people attend church to belong to a group where they can network and market themselves or their goods or services among people who will assume they are ethical and trustworthy due to the group inclusivity. Sort of religion as a BBB rating. A friend of mine chose a lawyer because he advertised in the church bulletin and he felt he could be trusted on that basis alone. (I checked him out online.) Politicians use religion ad nauseam to present a façade of trustworthiness and

honesty. This should be outlawed on the basis of separation of church and state. Political candidates should not even be allowed to mention religion.

5) Finally, people convince themselves that they believe, because the ready-made behavioral code of conduct is attractive to them. They don't have to think about what is right and wrong, it's all spelled out in the handbook. Like the driver's manual you study before your written driving test, memorize it and you're done. It's so easy. And occasionally you can get away with drifting through a stop sign without coming to a complete stop or committing adultery and all you have to do is pay a small penalty, feel remorse and promise not to do it again, until the next time you do it again.

To summarize, nobody really believes in god. They can't. It is simply impossible to really believe in a magical guy in the sky granting wishes and keeping track of us all, but they want to so badly, that they convince themselves they do, so that they can believe they are good, strong people, so that they have a social network, and so that they have a ready-made, group-endorsed code of conduct without going through the pesky process of thinking about it for themselves. Turns out humans don't really like to use their brains very much, they just enjoy bragging about how big their brains are, like an interspecies big brain contest.

Just think about that. Humans are too lazy to work out an ethical code for themselves, so they cling to a magic book that does it all for them. How un-American is that? Americans are supposed to believe in self sufficiency, doing things for yourself, facing the hard tasks and pulling yourself up by your boot straps to accomplish what needs to be done. But for the really important stuff, like moral behavior, we'll just refer to a millennia-old book written by cross-eyed, inbred, old white men for the sole purpose of consolidating power over other people. Brilliant. And if you won't adhere to the magic book, they're not above shooting you over it. Just clinging to their guns and Bibles, like Barack said.

The evidence that they don't really believe is the vehemence with which they proselytize. They know they're not convincing anyone else, so who are they really trying to convince when they harangue others with their "witnessing" (badgering) about Jesus and god? They are trying hard to convince themselves! The things people say about their belief in and love of Jesus basically sound like an old-fashioned revival meeting. If you've ever attended one, it is literally an embarrassingly torrid, religious orgy of orgiastic histrionics (i.e. they're screamers). They literally sound and look like orgies. They're gross and mortifying for the participants. They should be less humiliated by attending an actual sex orgy.

Gundamentalists are just those 9-year-old children doubling down on their "belief" in Santa god. They are the immature, the un-evolved of society, without a responsible adult to tell them "the Santa story". If they weren't so destructive and harmful, one might feel sorry for them and even protective of them, as we do mentally challenged people and children. As it is, we are required to be vigilant about them, lest they force us into moronic, stifling, repressive theocracy, which is their ultimate goal.

Chapter 4- Maybe I'M God! NO! Have I taught you nothing!?

What would an ethical code look like if we actually used our big brains to work one out? What kind of social contract would work best? First, it would be based on mutual social progress (cooperation) and not individual hoarding (competition). This is actually just the liberal/progressive versus conservative/regressive political struggle. Conservatives want to insure that individuals can do whatever they want to hoard resources and not have to concern themselves with the misfortunes of others. They don't want to pay taxes for anything but armaments to protect their wealth and they especially don't want to pay for social safety net programs for other people.

They resent taxes as an imposition on their right to hoard wealth, but this is fraudulent, because they use more resources than average people and should pay more for public works. Jeff Bezos' Amazon vehicles use the roads and infrastructure far more than I do, but he wants to pay less taxes to support them than I do. Rich businesses get to write off their operating expenses, but individuals don't. Billionaires spend more money electing representatives who will support their unfair tax breaks than they'd probably have to spend on their fair share of taxes, but to them it's the principle of the thing- their privilege, their right to hoard as much as they want. They're just kind of mean.

The far right wing demonization of the words liberal and progressive must never be permitted. Consider the literal meaning of the word "liberal". It means generous. What does conservative mean? It means stingy. Progressive just means desiring to make progress toward a better social system. Regressive means wanting to take us back to a time when fewer people had privilege. Think of those simple but accurate definitions every time you hear the terms liberal, conservative and progressive. Liberal vs. conservative is literally generous vs. stingy. Words matter. Don't let the greedy people co-opt words for their evil machinations.

It's astounding that such a negative connotation has become attached to the word Socialism in the United States. Socialism literally means an economic system based on what's best for society or people. How is that bad? America has gotten more mileage out of socialists waiting in lines for things than is reasonable. People in Socialist countries have to wait for health care. People in Soviet Russia had to stand in bread lines. Have you tried making a doctor's appointment or been to a supermarket lately in the U.S.? Waiting and lines! It's the worst argument. Yes, of course, all systems have problems, because there are eight fucking BILLION of us! It has much less to do with the economic system than overpopulation.

Now, let's consider the literal definition of capitalism, which is an economic system based on what is best for the accumulation of capital or money or wealth. Somehow that's the more noble system in our American eyes? We prefer a system that's better for money than one that is better for people. Wow. It speaks volumes about our character that we ignore the literal meaning of these two words in order to maintain our exploitative system. Usually, words are so important that they can turn the tide of events.

During the Russian revolution, the Communists were called the Bolsheviks, which means bigger or more in Russian and the opposition were called the Mensheviks, which means smaller or less. Is it any wonder who won? The Bolsheviks were able to control the message with their words. It's pretty natural to want more rather than less, especially in highly classist societies like imperial Russia, where most people weren't able to meet their basic needs of food and shelter.

The Capitalism/Socialism dichotomy is the exact opposite. The more favorable word, Socialism or

Peopleism was constantly vilified by the west until it became associated with something negative, despite its actual meaning which became lost to Americans. Whereas the more negative word Capitalism or actually Moneyism was so revered in textbooks and public discourse that its literal meaning was also lost and it managed to turn into an exalted ideal associated with the only path to freedom, which is simply untrue- a society does not have to provide unrestricted rights to hoard in order to be free.

Just because a country has the word socialism in its title, doesn't mean it is socialist. Many dictatorships throw that term in their official name. North Korea's official name is the Democratic People's Republic of Korea. Does anyone believe it's either democratic or a republic? No. It's just their propaganda name. N. Korea is not socialist either, that's pretty obvious, but dumbasses on line use N. Korea as an example that socialism doesn't work!

There are good aspects to both socialism and capitalism. Capitalism encourages motivation to achieve, by offering incentive for work, but socialism restrains people from exploiting others' work. An idea that would reconcile the two is to put a cap on how much more one person's work could be worth than any other's within a company or organization. If we decided that no one could be more than 100 times more valuable than anyone else, for example, that would cap the salary of the highest paid employee at 100 times that of the lowest paid employee, by law. Pay includes all salaries, bonuses, stocks and other perks, so the CEO can't hide his remuneration in order to get around this law.

This is based on the natural egalitarianism in which we profess to believe. Since no one person could be more than 100 times smarter, harder working, more industrious, more skilled, or more able than another, then it is injustice to be paid more than 100 times what anyone else is earning. Either someone is getting more than they deserve or someone is getting less than they deserve. That is the definition of injustice. It must be stopped. The unbridled, unregulated capitalism that has wrought CEOs making 5000 times what their janitors make is unjust because no one can work 5000 times more than another person. I'm not even sure about 100 times. We'd have to vote on it- I just threw a nice, round number out there to make the point. It does seem however, for it to be possible for someone to be 5000 times more ruthless, more unscrupulous than other people, but we wouldn't advocate rewarding those traits, would we? Yet, we do.

This remuneration cap incentivizes CEOs and other high earners who are ambitious, to bring the rest of their co-workers along with them, because if a greedy CEO wants to make five million dollars in compensation, she will have to pay the lower paid staff $50,000.

Now, I can already hear people screeching hysterically about Bill Gates and Jeff Bezos, who both had really good ideas that worked out well for them and the rest of us, too. But they still aren't thousands of times more deserving than the rest of us. Of course, they should be rewarded for their excellently executed ideas, but they should not be allowed to become obscenely more rich than the workers who helped execute them. Jeff Bezos should give up his useless dick rockets and instead pay the warehouse workers who keep his company running, and not make them use their dicks to pee into water bottles. He is not that much better, smarter or harder working than them. He's an exploitive capitalist, and he shouldn't be allowed to be. (And by the way, his idea of colonizing the moon is absolute bull shit propaganda. It ain't gonna happen.) But Bezos is just one of many terrible examples of capitalist injustice.

And now for my tax code, if I was Queen of the World. I would have to tweak this with some knowledgeable economists before putting it into practice, but the idea is what I refer to as a graduated flat tax, with no loopholes, no write-offs, no depreciation. And again it refers to all forms of compensation for work- salaries, bonuses, commissions, stocks, interest, capital gains, and perks of all kinds. There is no way to hide income by changing the name of it, and if you try, you will be punished for breaking the very easy to understand law.

If you earn under $20,000 you owe no tax. (Teen workers rejoice.)
If you earn $20,001- $35,000, you owe 3% of your income.
If you earn $35,001- $50,000, you owe 8%.
If you earn $50,001- $60,000, you owe 10%.
If you earn $60,001- $70,000, you owe 15%.
If you earn $70,001- $75,000, you owe 20%.
If you earn $75,001- $80,000, you owe 25%.
If you earn $80,001- $100,000, you owe 30%.
If you earn $100,001- $400,000, you owe 35%.
If you earn more than $400,000, you owe 40%.

Corporations and businesses taking in more than $400,000 pay 45%, less than $400,000 will pay according to above schedule. If you have a small business which is your only income, you don't have to pay twice.

Built into this tax code would be the need to revisit it every few years, as salaries and cost of living changed, but that is the general idea. Clearly, I'm no economist, but I said it would have to be tweaked by professionals.

Churches will be taxed as the businesses they are. They may garner deductions for performing non-religious public service, such as soup kitchens or shelters, as long as you don't have to pray or be preached at to use those services. But honestly, they should want to do those things out of the goodness of their hearts without any monetary incentive, so maybe they won't get tax credits. I expect when churches cease being instruments of control for the wealthy and sources of prestige for the masses, they'll fade away. Then, we'll use their fantastic buildings for something useful like animal shelters and public gathering halls. What a great day that will be.

There will definitely be no tax breaks for overpopulating the world. One child will be the standard tax rate and due to our extreme overpopulation, couples should currently be encouraged to have just one child at most. And that's not one child per marriage, it's one child per couple, one time. Choose wisely, because whoever you breed with, that's your choice, but if you get remarried and breed some more, it's going to cost you.

So, the base tax rate is for one child. Your second child doubles your taxes, third child triples them, etc. Family benefits paid out to families in need will also be based on one child and not increased for additional children. All children will be provided free meals at school, however, so that every child's brain can develop optimally. So, your kids will eat if you over breed and overburden yourself with taxes, but you may not be able to afford cable TV or a car. People who don't have any kids get a nice, big tax break.

If a couple in a second marriage have a second child each, they both double their taxes. If one spouse does not have another child, that spouse's taxes remain the same and only the offending spouse with the second child gets doubled taxes. Imagine if they both already had a kid though and are paying child support, too. In other words, choose wisely the first time, and don't keep having kids, because you'll be broke, you'll stay broke, and you'll hate life even more than parents do now. (I know nobody admits the drudgery of raising kids, but you're just not being honest with yourselves. It's self preservation.)

Now, I know you think this sounds cruel and punitive, but again it's actually just a matter of justice. Families with more children use more resources and should therefore have to pay more. They use more food, water, education, facilities, resources, and more than their share of everything, so it's only fair they pay more.

It will quickly become tres déclassé to even consider having more than one child. Also, it will become normalized to decide not to have children. The social pressure to breed will dwindle away.

But how will this affect the world economy? I am mystified by the economic trope that economies must always be growing in order to be healthy. Would we think it healthy if humans or other animals just continued to grow indefinitely? No. Each generation, the human population will be halved, and hysterical conservatives, we will have managed to do it without genocide or death panels or eugenics or any of the gonadical (testosteronical? the male version of hysterical, since it's always men screeching about this) ravings which attend any attempt at human population curtailment.

With the population halved each generation, there will be less need for goods and services, commensurate with the fewer workers to provide them. The fact that Earth's resources are being depleted at a much slower rate will create a state of plenty, which in turn will make sharing more amenable. Cooperation can replace competition for resources.

The planet will be nurtured and respected as to resource extraction, because humans won't need as much from her. And can we just lay off mining gemstones altogether? Why do you need a shiny rock? We can make them. We made self-parking cars, Christmas lights and cubic zirconia, we can make shiny rocks galore. Anyway, resources can be extracted at a safe, leisurely, deliberately thoughtful pace.

Earth's resources must be commonly held, so that greed cannot be a factor in their disbursal. The cost of natural resources will be equal to the cost of retrieval, transport, and refinement, which will include respectable salaries for the workers who do it. This will create good, safe jobs, but no obscene profits for greedy, evil oil barons, like the sociopathic Bushes and the Rockefellers. The only reason oil companies ostensibly own oil is because they have the guns to hoard it. And it's not even their guns, they're our tax payer bought guns held by our military, most of whom are stationed in areas where resources, especially oil need protection. It takes guns and violence to hoard something that comes naturally from the planet for all.

We must abolish wage slavery. People need to have lives that are a good balance between working hard to get things accomplished and having free time to enjoy doing what they prefer. Working 40 hours per week (which really equals more like 50 hrs/week with travel and prep time), 50 weeks per year does not provide this. We need to immediately go to a 30 hour work week, some of which can be done from home. This is the only positive outcome of the recent pandemic, the new realization that work can be done without a monotonous commute. Production will stay the same because workers will be more energized and enthusiastic about their work if they don't have to devote all their time to it, so that a greedy boss can make more money from their labor.

Life is made up of time. If you have to sell most of your time to an exploitative employer, you are selling your life away. It is a terrible waste of life. It is an injustice. It is wage slavery.

If all went well, we could actually take the work week down to 25 hours. I could easily accomplish my job in 25 or 30 hours per week, if they just eliminated all the useless meetings and time consuming busy work. The only thing that is affected by the reduction of hours in the work week, is coverage, and this can be resolved by staggering workers' hours, and in the case of small businesses where coverage is maintained by single minimum wage employees, just adding another shift. Yeah, the greedy employer might have to pay a bit more. Or cover the shift himself.

There would have to be a law which forbade employers firing employees at the beginning of this new system to hire new employees at a lower rate of pay. Heavy fine or punishment if they tried.

There would need to be at least one four day weekend per month. I suggest MLK Day as the January four-day weekend, the Monday closest to Valentine's Day in February, the Friday closest to International Women's Day and my Mom's birthday, a born feminist, (March 8th and 9th respectively) for March, the Monday closest to April 15th as the Spring Holiday, Memorial Day for May, the Friday closest to Summer Solstice for June, July 4th and the Friday closest to July 15th or

Midsummer for July, the closest Monday to August 15th for the Summer Holiday, Labor Day for September, the Friday closest to October 15th for Autumn Leaves Day, Thanksgiving and the Friday after, for November, and of course, the long Solstice/Christmas/Chanukah/Ramadan/Kwanzaa/New Year's Holiday from December 21st to January 2nd for the Winter Holiday. This is a schedule humans could look forward to and know they were working for something not only that contributed to society, but also gave them a sense of freedom and well-being.

Also, everyone must get a minimum 4 weeks paid vacation per year after being in a job one year and it would increase to 5 weeks after 5 years at the job, 6 weeks after 10 years on the job, 7 weeks after 15 years, and max out at 8 weeks after 20 years at the same job. This gives incentive to stay at one position and gain experience and institutional knowledge, thereby increasing expertise and productivity.

Seniority would matter. In order to minimize favoritism and sycophantism, all privileges must be based on longevity in the job, to include but not be limited to: choice of office space, if applicable, choice of work hours or shift if applicable, priority in vacation time selection, and order of lay-offs if this occurred, i.e. last to be hired, first to be fired.

These steps would pretty much eliminate the wage slavery that most of us experience today.

Speaking of abolishing slavery, we must abolish animal slavery. Animals are not ours to eat, wear, experiment on, use for entertainment, or enslave.

Animals, for sure, have personalities, which should give them legal status as persons. So, animals are people, too. Unlike sociopaths, they have consciences. Evidence abounds- the gorilla who gently carried the human child who had fallen into her enclosure to the door and handed him to the zoo keeper, dogs who rescue humans and other animals, lactating animals who nurse orphans, even of other species (watch You Tube). The male gorilla who tried to use a child who fell into his enclosure as a toy (who was immediately shot and killed by humans) was possibly the donald trump of gorillas, stupid and mean, or maybe he was just trying to playfully rough house with the kid, as dads do, and didn't realize his strength relative to the child.

Also, animals clearly feel love as much as humans. Again, there are countless videos of animals snuggling together, putting their arms around each other, grooming each other, kissing, even mourning loved ones. You simply cannot dismiss it as happenstance and coincidence, no matter how badly you want to think they have no feelings, so you won't feel guilty eating them, you Atheist murderers. Oh, take it like a woman, you know I'm right.

That's why I was pretty offended when Robert DeNiro called trump a pig and a dog. I understood his intent was to insult trump, but he actually insulted pigs and dogs, who are better people than trump. Next time he wants to insult trump, first of all he should go with something not alive, like garbage or sewage, but even garbage and sewage play an important role in sanitation, so even they are more useful than the sociopath trump. Whenever I reach as low as I can to insult trump, no matter what it is, I add, "With apologies to garbage or sewage", or whatever I call him, because he is the lowest thing I can think of. Does that thing (trump) have any value at all? I think not. What has he (it) ever contributed to the world or humanity? Nothing. It just takes up space and wastes resources, and gives nothing back. Sorry, but cheesy skyscrapers built by others, many of whom weren't paid, don't count.

So, we must quit eating other persons of other species. Meat must be phased out as previously stressed. This can be gradual and as gentle as possible, but sooner rather than later. It's really a simple matter of what grocery stores and restaurants offer. I promise you, you will still eat wonderfully and thrillingly. Food will still be a highlight of any day. People will feel better because their digestive systems will no longer be stressed and clogged by processing corpses through their bowels. You will feel lighter both physically and psychologically, not being burdened by the guilt of cannibalizing your fellow Earthlings.

You may not think you feel guilty, but you do. That's why people are so hostile to vegetarians and vegans. You know you shouldn't eat your fellow animals, but you want to and the mere existence of vegans makes you realize it can be done, and makes you feel guilty and acutely aware of your lack of will power to do what you know is right. You claim we vegans are obnoxiously sanctimonious (and granted, I am being a little here because it's necessary to make the point), but we don't even have to say anything except that we don't eat meat and you automatically extrapolate that we feel superior to you and you feel anger and guilt. And remember, if you eat meat, you are rejecting god's purpose for us, to fix the food chain mistake, so you are an Atheist.

No fur, leather, sheepskin, or down can be used, human-made materials only, from here on out. Those human-made goods will be outstanding, because, you know, we're the species who built superhighways, electric cars, and smart phones, so we're pretty competent.

Animal experimentation ends immediately. All lab animals must be provided any necessary remedial healthcare and turned over to a facility where they can live out cushy, comfortable lives with all their needs met. Churches could be better used in this way.

No circus animal acts, animal shows or non-habitat, non-rescue zoos will be permitted.

All pets must have the status of family members. That means they live indoors in the family space. They have freedom like other family members, they are trained to live harmoniously in the family home, and they are never chained outside for lengthy periods, but can be walked on a leash and halter within the neighborhood or a park, where their human is responsible to clean up after them. I expect pet trainers to be very wealthy, high-status citizens in this perfected society, as their skills will be in very high demand, just like the yoga instructors in the chocolate scenario.

There will be no pack animals, no draft animals, or even service animals, unless the animal is treated like a family member, and I think it goes without saying there will be no bomb-sniffing dogs, mine-sweeping dolphins or any other task that a human would not be asked to perform.

Surely, I do not need to reiterate, even though I will, that men and macho women will not be allowed to hunt animals to make their dicks feel bigger. However, if they really feel a need to hunt, they may hunt *each other* in closed, domed hunting facilities, bereft of any other living plant or animal to shoot up and then they can just go to town with their AR-15s, on each other. Maybe they will need the written permission of their wives or mothers. Animal population will be controlled with birth control methods, like the human animals. Maybe hunters could use their skills to shoot birth control injections into animals.

Next. OK, here we go. The Fucking Patriarchy must be extinguished with such extreme prejudice that it will never be able to rear its ugly head again. Ever, ever, ever. Here's a brief history of the fucking patriarchy: Males are biologically bigger than females, so they bully females. The primitive mind believes that might makes right. It's that simple. Men are that simple.

They have always raped and threatened females with physical violence and harm or even death if the females would not do their bidding. Then, when men began to form societies, they made all the rules, all the foundational myths such as gods, and all the social systems to benefit the males. And if women didn't go along with it, they would be harmed or killed.

The myths served to internalize the rules and social systems and eventually women began to believe

they were inferior to men. Like the Eve and Adam myth
made the female the evil one (for wanting to gain
knowledge, no less, that's how dumb religion wants to
keep us). The early Hebrews and still some orthodox
religionists today were positively obsessed with
women's menstruation being unclean, literally
ostracizing and sequestering them at that time of their
cycle. But somehow those filthy dicks that they'll stick
into anything were never considered this way, although
they did have a bit of a preoccupation about where
semen could be discharged (like the weirdo "Proud"
Boys of today).

Primitive religionists tagged sex as dirty because
they only knew it as a bodily function for rape and
reproduction. Sex actually *is* dirty when it is severed
from love and intimacy, because you're exchanging
bodily fluids like cum, sweat, and saliva, so it's basically
sharing dirt, especially before modern hygiene. Why
would you want to do that with anyone except someone
you love?

While watching a Hallmark Christmas movie, it
occurred to me that they omit any hint of sex, ostensibly
to remain wholesome, their religious roots poking
through. Which begs the question, do they not consider
sex between loving adults wholesome? Or are their
couples not as loving as they'd have us believe? Do they
really believe in love or just use it as a fictional plot

device to entertain women? Just kidding, I love Hallmark movies for their elaborate Christmas decorations, and the chaste kisses are enough to convey the idea. And occasionally, there's even a good storyline. So, yeah, the love is just a plot device to entertain women. And it works. But those tens of thousands of dollars worth of decorations outrank the romance, because most of us can't afford that for our homes, whereas we have all experienced the big, old disappointment that is romance.

Anyway, I'm not exactly sure why sex became such an obsession for religionists but I have a couple of theories. One, in order to maintain complete control of populations and especially women, you have to be able to control the means of reproduction, so naturally when men were inventing god and his supposed rules, sex had to be tightly regulated. You didn't want your enemies to outnumber you, so you had to keep women cranking out allies. This was true when humans were wandering bands of hunters/foragers and then especially true after agriculture became the main economic system- women had to produce farm workers. Also, you wanted to make sure you weren't spending your wealth, time, and energy raising someone else's progeny, so there had to be strict rules about women's virginity, chastity and faithfulness with fearsome penalties for disobedience. There were no such rules for men.

My second theory is that people are awfully intimidated by sex. Men are afraid they're not that good at it, and many are not, so they made rules about it- how you had to do it, when you could do it, how often you did it, where, when and why you were allowed to do it, until they managed to make it so constrained that it seemed perfunctory. They definitely succeeded in removing any joy from it for women, for I don't know, millennia! That way, if women didn't know they were supposed to enjoy it, they wouldn't know the difference when a man was really bad at it. But the tribe would keep on outnumbering the enemies.

When the Women's Movement began in the early 20th century, it had few members. It often cost women everything, including their lives to participate, so only the bravest few did so. Then, in the sixties, after basically keeping the country running during WW2, but then being shooed back to their kitchens so the men could have their jobs back and be the kings of their castles again lording financial security over women, women began to get restless. They'd had a taste of having control over their own finances and lives and they didn't necessarily revel in being subordinated in their households again. They began gathering in those kitchens and started talking, and lo and behold, they discovered that they weren't the only disgruntled, good, little housewives. Lots of women were dissatisfied.

They kept talking, they organized and they made progress in many areas. But here's where they failed. They actually never managed to get equal power in their households. The men were still the kings of the castle (or the shack, the trailer, the Cape Cod, or whatever). If both adults in the home worked, the woman was still responsible for all the family work. She still came home from a long day at work and cooked dinner, she still got the kids ready for school the next day, she still kept the house clean. Men still came home and asked, "What's for dinner?", then sat down in front of the TV with their newspaper.

Why did women allow this? Well, I understand it's quite a bit better now in the younger generations, those young men having been raised mostly by single moms who taught them better (pointed out by my sister), but it still occurs. The way men get women to do all the work is to just not do it. Most women raising children are not going to let the children go unfed, live in a filthy house, not do their homework and not have decent clothes to wear to school. So, they do what needs to be done, the family work. The men act magnanimous when they cook a meal on the grill once in a blue moon and think they've "helped".

Men are willing to live in squalor and often do when living alone or with other men. They just don't do what they perceive to be women's work. So, when they move in with a woman, they just continue to not do it, and the woman does because women can't live with dirty clothes strewn all over the floor. Young women of today have a term for this: intentional incompetence, I believe. What normal-intelligence person can't do laundry or clean a house?

Granted, this is not all men, but in the first generation of proto-Feminists, you'd be shocked at how many lived this way. It's almost as though they acted like the men "allowed" them to work, and they were so grateful that they didn't want to rock the boat and speak up about the imbalance of labor. Women generally prefer peace to conflict and so they pick their battles carefully. They don't want to fight over every, single, thoughtless transgression that men commit, because they'd be fighting all the time. God forbid, they'd seem like nags!

This is also why those god-awful hyphenated names have become so prevalent. Men don't mind complaining when they don't like something, so they whine if women attempt to keep their perfectly good original names. Hyphenated names are NOT Feminist! Just the opposite, they demonstrate that a woman didn't have the fortitude to face her whining male and tell him directly and firmly, "I already have a name, I don't need another one." Nothing says weakness like a hyphenated name. They're also damned inconvenient for everyone else: They don't fit on forms, they're a waste of breath to say, they're annoying to write out, and they need to go.

It was horrifying to see Congresswomen referred to as "Mrs." in the January 6th committee hearings. The unmarried women had "Ms." on their name plates, but the married ones had "Mrs." What the fuck?! How is that any different than Miss and Mrs? These are **Congresswomen!** They are all Ms! In some cases, Dr.! What does their marital status have to do with their work? Mrs. must be eliminated. How are we still using it sixty years after the Feminist Movement gave us Ms!? As long as there is but one title for men both married and unmarried, there must only be one for women. These details matter. Words **matter**!

The only names that should be hyphenated are the family names in a household, where the girls should have the last name of their mother and the boys can have the last name of their father if he's still in the picture. Then, that family can be the Smith-Jones family, but the girls are Smiths and the boys are Joneses. The hyphenated name nonsense is emblematic of the compromises women have made to Feminist philosophy. Women should keep their own name, they should require partners to do their fair share of family work, and they should damn well expect to have orgasms. If any "Proud" Boys were to read this, their balls would recede back up into their groin, but I'm sure they can't read it.

In the early days of the Feminist movement, an important tenet was to not blame the victims, the women, for their own plight. This certainly makes sense and was a good principle at the time, because people can't help their socialization. Sixty years later, when we're still fighting the same battles with men for pay equity, power equality in relationships, bodily autonomy, and the right to not be harassed by horny assholes, it's time to take a more proactive stand and maybe even admit we've been too nice and too passive. Maybe it's time to get a lot tougher on bad men. Maybe we **are** enabling our own victimization, and it's time to take responsibility for our own passivity, and change it! We may have to accept being a bit unpleasant to accomplish this. So what? They're going to call us shrews and nags anyway, so we may as well do what we have to do to get our equality.

I'm not even just talking about the tiny-dicked Tucker Carlsons, Steve Bannons and Steven Millers of the world who are so gynophobic that they're actually jokes, but also the basically nice men who just don't want to be bothered with women's emotions, don't want to do their fair share of family work (half!), and think of sex as "smashing" (I'm talking to you, Trevor Noah) or banging. Women don't want to be smashed and banged, I guarantee you. They just go along with these labels, so as not to seem nitpicky.

Women, don't let men turn lovemaking into banging. Don't let men convince you that you want to smash, when what you really want is to meld with someone you love. Don't let men control what sex is, since they are wrong about almost everything and definitely wrong in this case. Don't let them turn love into an athletic event, which is just a game and doesn't mean anything (even though sports seem to be the only thing men are allowed to emote over). Don't let men convince you that you're work-out equipment! Women must keep men from defining sex, or sex remains just another casualty of sexism.

There was a movie populated by millennial characters in which the two protagonists finally established they were in love, and the man said to the woman, "I'm gonna fuck the shit out of you." (Shame on you, Adam Scott!) That's an actual quote from an actual movie that was actually supposed to be about actual love. Ewwww! First of all, just the literal meaning of that, should *never* be permitted to intrude in any romantic scene that most women would want to be involved in. The line should have been, "I'm gonna kiss you and make love to you so intensely, so gently, so appreciatively, so emotionally and so passionately." Which obviously would have led to sex unless one of them was on their way to work! So, why wasn't the correct dialogue filmed? Too feminine? Too corny? The horrible line was in there because, as usual, the idea of love had to be subsumed to male priorities. And I think a woman produced that movie!

I understand that the line was meant to convey his great passion for her, but it didn't, any more than violence demonstrates passion, which we practically accept without question in pop culture. When animals copulate, it often looks exactly the same as fighting, so it seems natural to mistake violence for passion, but again, that's what our big brains are for- to figure out how to do better! Since men's brains are between their legs, I guess it's up to us women to use *our* brains and teach men that violence and love do not go together.

Passion does not equal violence. If a man feels the need to be rough or even vigorous, to smash or bang, he is not feeling passion, he is feeling power. That is why they have conditioned women to think of passion as violent, so they could enjoy feeling power, which they love and aspire to, while the woman is deceived into believing she is experiencing great passion. How does pounding away on someone express love? It does not. It expresses and demonstrates only power.

Women became Feminist and decided they could be just as sexual as men are, which is accurate, but it led to emulating male sexual behavior which had already been established by men as competitive and an act of physical prowess. Where was the emotional prowess that women value? Women want to meld, not smash; we want to blend, not bang; we want to love each other, not nail each other. Women must take sex back for themselves and decide what *they* want it to be, not just accept the male-established version of it. Don't let men define what great sex is- they get everything wrong, because they rank everything according to physical strength, going back to their cave man days. It's time for women to have these conflicts, risk being called nags, and get what we want and our fair share of power (half!).

I keep saying half for our share of the power because we have had a tendency to accept whatever crumbs of power men have tossed to us and been thankful. Feminism isn't about subjugating men. Men only think that because they assume we will do to them what they have done to us when we get power. That's also why racists are so afraid of Black people getting power, why all the trumpster trash lost their minds over a half-black president being elected. All Feminists want is our fair share of power, which is half in any relationship, perhaps more in society in general, commensurate with our larger numbers. And by the way, that's all Black people want, too, their fair share of power (but they can't help having bigger dicks than you, little Tucker and Donnie). But just a word of caution, rabidly violent racist-gynophobes; you keep pushing other groups to the extent of taking away their rights, suppressing their votes, shooting them in the back when they're unarmed, and making laws to oppress them, and they will eventually get really pissed, and then they might just feel vengeful when they get power and be as nasty to you as you were to them!

The main reason Feminism didn't realize its early ideals is that women are much more desperate (yes, I am standing by that word) for relationships than men are, due to our millennia of socialization. Men know this and they exploit it. Women have to be willing to make a fulfilling life on their own and forego reproducing rather than accept unequal relationships, and so far we have not.

In popular culture single men are portrayed as lucky and free, while single women are portrayed as desperate and incomplete. Women are called "the old ball and chain". We laugh it off. It's not OK. Again, it internalizes this idea that somehow men have more value than women. If a woman finds out that her fiancé called her the ball and chain at his bachelor party, she should call off the wedding. Women laugh such insults off because they don't want to seem humorless, they want to be perceived as one of the guys and pretend to be in on the joke. That is not being in on the joke; that is being the butt of the joke. Men mean it when they say such things about women, the light tone is to make it seem neutral, like when trump says something threatening and tries to claim it was said in jest.

Another desperate thing women do to rationalize unequal relationships is that they delude themselves into believing that they do have all the power in the relationship. I can't tell you how many women I have heard say that women have all the power. That is a delusional statement! If you are doing more than half of the family work (cooking, cleaning, childcare, etc), you do not have power. You are a servant. If you have all your money in a joint account and you find your partner has his own bank account (which most men do, it's the girlfriend/golf/saloon account), you do not have power. These delusions and the acceptance of these indignities allow you to live a peaceful life, but they also allow men to maintain the status quo in their favor, and this is why sixty years later, we are *losing* civil rights and still living as second class citizens. How many times do we have to fight the same abortion issues, or have another Me Too movement?

Another reason the Feminist movement didn't fulfill its potential is that it got stuck in the ivory towers and neglected to normalize Feminism through pop culture, and also neglected women of color in the movement. The Gay Rights movement is the best example of rapid cultural change in modern history. Feminists hold symposiums at universities where they are basically preaching to the choir all the time. Gay people got out there and wrote such entertaining TV shows, movies and books that people began to realize they may know and love someone just like Will from Will and Grace, and that made them also see how wonderful Jack was. Ellen was already beloved when she came out, and she brought a lot of ignorant people around to the fact that someone's sexual orientation doesn't define their value (also, it's none of your goddamned business and what's wrong with you that you're so interested in other people's sex lives, you pervs!).

Pop culture helps to frame what's OK for people. Feminism ignored pop culture, to its detriment. Sorry, but these pop culture "Feminists", where the independent woman's main goal is still finding her man, is NOT enlightening or instructive. Where are the Feminist characters in TV and movies who are willing to forego marriage and children until men improve? (And, I'm sorry, fifty different versions of Uma Thurman kicking ass in a sexy body suit doesn't count.) The fictional so-called Feminists make the same compromises that real women do- they're constantly on the hunt for a man. They compromise too much for a man. Now, I know that everyone agrees that compromise is part of being in a relationship, but again, if a woman is doing more than half the compromising in a relationship, she is abdicating power.

In pop culture, they get around this by creating fictional men who are so loving and sensitive and perfect that either no compromise is necessary or the men do their fair share of it. But this is not portraying the reality for Feminist women. There is no such thing as a truly Feminist TV show, movie or even novel that I'm aware of, because it's too easy to dream up fictional Feminist men to resolve the Feminist romantic tension. I used to love Barbara Kingsolver's stories, but every Feminist dilemma was resolved by the introduction of an unrealistically Feminist man. All cozy mysteries starring women employ this literary device. Where are all these square-jawed, handsome, sexually adept, ostensibly Feminist men? Well, they seem to be confined to books and shows. Where are the sitcoms and movies about women who brook no bullshit from men and would rather be alone? Because that's where women are right now, **without** a sufficient supply of available, Feminist men.

This situation does not help to normalize truly Feminist behavior. Instead it keeps women hopeful that they, too, will find one of these fictional Feminist men and when they don't, the social imperative to breed and raise children with a partner compels them to settle and over-compromise, forestalling any meaningful alteration of the social contract and keeping men in charge.

Women want that happy-ever-after, true love, soulmate level of romance. We know that for sure because of the romance novels they read and write, the soap operas, TV shows and movies they watch and make, the songs they write and listen to. It is indisputable that women want this. But men don't. They think true love effeminizes them, weakens them. That's why they're uncomfortable with demonstrating loving emotions. Women think love strengthens them. (And not because of the added muscle mass in the person of the male partner.) They know it strengthens them psychologically and emotionally.

What women want out of love is for someone to get to know everything about them and like all of it. They want to be fully appreciated. They want someone to always have their back, even in the face of disapproving in-laws. And women want to give that all back to their partner in equal measure, but they can't, when all their partner does is act macho and indifferent until he's horny. Then women get resentful because their emotional needs are not being met and the relationship devolves into sniping at each other. (Women who want power more than love have just assimilated to the masculine way of competition to survive.)

Men basically want sex. A warm garage for their dick. Because they've been taught that's what they want. They've been unfortunately socialized, too.

We need romance novels that are more than bodice rippers, populated by para-rapists with throbbing members. We need stories in which men tell women how wonderful they are, not by citing their silken hair, succulent breasts and creamy thighs, but instead praising their specific intelligent ideas, strength of character, kind thoughts and actions, and stimulating conversation. Likewise, women must appreciate those characteristics in men. It's OK to like that throbbing member or those succulent breasts sometimes, but to make them the focal point of romance is just inaccurate and inappropriate.

Men make romantic literature, film, music and art, too, but they don't believe their own words, so one can draw the conclusion that their motives are collectively to keep women believing in them, to keep women wanting men's scant emotions, and to keep women accepting the crumbs of love men brush from their table, with the obscure hope of true love. To keep women hoping for great love but in the process be willing to settle for less than they want. Basically, to keep the fairy tale alive that keeps the sex and offspring flowing.

So, men act like they can take love or leave it, take women or leave them. And they can take it or leave it, romance that is, not sex. They think sex is a basic need, like food, water and shelter. Thanks, Maslow, the one time he went all Freud on us. Whenever a man whines that he's lonely, it usually means he's horny. You can argue that that's just my opinion, but try starting a relationship with a man without engaging in sex for what they think is too long a time, and you will quickly feel your hair blowing in the windy wake of his hasty departure. You know, that thing where a man pretends he's OK with being "just friends" in hopes you'll get horny and screw him, and when you don't, suddenly your good friend is pissed off and a friend no more.

By the way, it's a lie that men **need** sex and it hurts them if they don't get it when they are aroused (the myth of blue balls). I know this for a fact because I withheld sex from **a lot** of excited men (almost a scientific sampling) and exactly zero of them died or even had any long lasting repercussions, except for bruised egos. The poor babies were uncomfortable for a bit. (I'd love to quip, "You guys know who you are", but they're probably all dead by now as I specialized in older men and I'm already pretty old.) . That lie (the blue balls myth) is just more of men's selfish pursuit of winning, the result of competitive culture. Men lie about blue balls to take advantage of women's nurturing instincts to win, like it's a game they need to win to feel good about themselves.

But meanwhile, men are allowed to get women all worked up about love and then withhold it. And women have had real consequences from that- they've died, been depressed, gotten ill, had their lives ruined. But that's not considered as bad as withholding sex! Maybe there should be a special epithet for men who let women down in love, like heart-tease. But look how much gentler that sounds than dick-tease? You wouldn't want to be too hard on men! How about dick-bitch, as in you're a bitch to your dick?

While women want true, eternal love, men want to reduce love to a biological function, another act of competition: power, prowess, and procreation. Men have something to prove: look how long I can go, look how many times I can do it, look how big it is. Women are not exercise equipment! Sex is not a work out! A man never tells his buddies how long he gazed into her eyes, how much they cuddled or kissed. His male friends would laugh at him and call him a pussy, insinuate that he was feminized and demeaned by real feelings. Even nice, loving men know better than to talk about love with their buddies.

So, women and men want two different things. Who wins? Well, obviously men do, so far; they have convinced women that their romantic expectations are unrealistic and over the top. They should accept the pittance of love that men want to dole out to them and be satisfied. Grow up. Be realistic. Settle. You had that romantic proposal, where I kneeled before you for 30 seconds, so I could have you under my thumb forever. That should hold you for life. That gives you something to tell your girlfriends. What if women treated sex that way and told men to be realistic- you had that great sex on our honeymoon; that should hold you for life and gives you something to tell your boyfriends.

Women, gentle people who prefer not to always be in conflict, and have a predilection for cooperation rather than competition will always feel they should compromise to get to a solution to a problem. But men have a tendency toward competition. They want to **win** the argument and have their own way. And feel powerful.

Well, what's wrong with that? Perfect system, right? Like the food chain. Women feel good about compromising and men like to win. Perfect fit, like yin and yang, prey and predator. Except for two things: 1) this sort of lopsided compromise ruins love and relationships, because it's a hierarchy of two and she's below him on that hierarchy. Nobody wants to be the low woman on the totem pole. It makes you mad. That's why so many women constantly bitch about their relationships and why many divorced women never marry again. It's also why so many marriages that do last, just turn into bad habits. And 2) What if Women's Way of Cooperation is the right way to move the world forward? (Spoiler alert: it is.) Male rule and the male way of competition has forever wrought on the Earth war, violence, cruelty, discord, destruction, despair, dominance, slavery, misery, and fear. A new feminized cooperative approach is the humanity-saving change we need.

Aren't we women then remiss to simply acquiesce to the incorrect male way of competition that leads to human disaster, to simply give in and compromise to keep the peace? Don't we have an obligation to improve humanity by teaching and inspiring people to adopt a feminine, cooperative approach to social living, which leads to generosity, and bringing everyone along at a similar pace of progress so there need not be conflict, injustice, or want? Even if culture advances a bit more slowly. You might not have as many cathedrals, skyscrapers, or gadgets, but on the flip side, you might not have war, poverty, and hatred either, if cooperation replaced competition.

Competitors rank everything and everyone, so they create hierarchies, thus the sexist hierarchy that places women below men in men's minds and even many women's. Let me explain how ugly this is to men in terms they can understand: You know how devastated the losing team in the Super Bowl is, after the big game? So dejected that they came in second in the whole country? How disappointing it is to be a silver medalist in the Olympics, despite how talented they were at their sport? Well, that's how women feel *all the time*. We don't like being in second place anymore than your favorite athlete.

Pop culture defines masculinity and femininity and it takes too much energy to buck conformity. So, most men don't reject the accepted tenets of masculinity, which has the extra, added appeal of placing them in an advantageous position. But why do so many women internalize their own gender inferiority or subjugate their legitimate emotions?

Well, once you've believed something for millennia, Jung's collective unconsciousness kicks in and it seems like an integral part of life, something that's always been there and always will be. It comes to seem innate. Many people think that gender behavioral traits are innate. They are not. They are learned. They are inculcated by men into women through millennia of sexism and oppression: that women are more vulnerable and need protection; that women are and should be more nurturing and loving, that women are weaker; that women need love more than men, that women need children, that women are submissive, that women need men… Women have a millennia-long case of Stockholm Syndrome!

Let's say for the sake of argument that there were innate gender traits, i.e. that women were more emotional than men and prioritized love over sex, and men were more physical and prioritized sex over love. What's wrong with that? That should be fine, right? Just different, but complimentary. Yin and yang. Pop quiz! What is wrong with that scenario?

    A.) Hierarchy
    B.) Ranking
    C.) Sexism
    D.) All of the above

Of course, the answer is D. In the competition-driven, male-created hierarchy built illegitimately from their larger size and strength, males and male things outrank females and female things, rendering emotionality and romance inferior to physicality and sex. Psychologist Carol Gilligan pointed this out decades ago, although she framed it more politically than emotionally, but again, it has remained mostly in the ivory towers.

So, the differences in perspective between women and men are not the problem. The ranking of the differences are. If women and men considered female and male traits equal in rank, the differences could be charming. Women would want lots of love and open affection and men would too, if they didn't have to worry about displaying a "submissive", low-ranked, effeminate trait. Conversely, men would still crave lots of sex, and women would too, if they didn't have to feel like they were being dominated by men who weren't even loving enough to do their fair share of both the family work and the sex effort.

Women being more emotional and men being more physical could actually be enchanting because without the inequality they would complement each other and cover the bases, not conflict with each other as they do now in the hierarchy. And so would femininity and masculinity. Wouldn't that be nice? (Or do humans just love the drama of incompatibility and I'm just a starry-eyed optimist who craves harmony? Nah. Harmony is innately positive.) If men could access their emotions as deeply as women, women could access their sexuality as profoundly as men, and men would find their dicks much more cheerfully attended to. Both emotion and physicality are good. Equality is good. There is no justification for ranking, which is the result of a male-created competitive system and the basis for hierarchy and sexism. It isn't necessary nor does it provide any advantage for humanity. The only purpose of ranking is to create power, and power is not a legitimately positive value.

Living with sexism for the entirety of human history is like existing in a blurry world. Everything is perceived through a sexist, blurry filter, like Vaseline on glass, and is skewed by it. We get used to the blur and believe it to be normal, innate even. We've been seeing society through the blurry filter of competitiveness, hierarchy and sexism our entire existence, causing us to compete and rank rather than cooperate, until we came to think it was the natural order of things. But even if it is the natural order as observed in nature, it is an inferior system. We can do better and must. That is what our big brains are for! Are we not smart enough to revise the flawed natural order and evolve? Isn't that our entire reason for being?

In our defense, we have been trying to adjust our focus for a few mere decades, but if you were keeping track of our progress on one of those giant fund raiser thermometer thingies, you would find only a thin, red line barely rising from the bottom. So, we have to do better. Sexism must be exterminated (not men, drop your balls back down, little Tucker, it's not the same thing, but you think it takes exterminating men to eliminate sexism because you're so committed to your feigned superiority, you assume all men are).

Eradicating sexism is as urgent as dealing with climate change. No one is ever going to experience real love until sexism is exterminated. Don't bother to protest. You don't love someone if you put yourself above them. Every little sexist law that is passed, attitude that is expressed, custom that is maintained keeps women beneath their male partners. Men's consent to these things implies tacit approval of sexism.

Most men aren't trying to be sexist and don't even think they are. They are just acting the way they've been taught. But if they've ever even gently cajoled a woman about having sex with them, they were being sexist as hell. Do they think we women don't know whether we want to have sex or not? They need to inform us? I dated a guy who was quite the cajoler, and at the end of his unsuccessful badgering, he was very disappointed (though no Lotharios were harmed in the making of this scenario). I said to him, "I told you from the beginning we weren't going to have sex." He responded, "Yeah, but that's just what all girls say so they look like nice girls," the jackassery of which statement was so profound, I have remembered it for over half a century. His extremely un-nuanced approach reminds me of republicans who want to outlaw abortion, maybe even birth control, remove any social safety networks which might help with any ill-conceived offspring, but who still intend to constantly harass women for sex, deny it's theirs if a pregnancy occurs, and feel nothing for the resulting child.

If a man has ever interrupted what a woman was saying because he thought his own comments were more important, he was being sexist. If he ever tuned a woman out to listen to what another man had to say, he was being sexist. If he ever declined to do half of the family work (childcare, housecleaning and meal prep), he was being sexist. Most, if not all men have committed these sexist infractions, whether they realize it or not. Watch a meeting sometime and see whose ideas are addressed and whose are ignored, and you will observe sexism in play, often even in pink collar settings.

Some men are beginning to object to sexism, but bless their hearts (which I mean in the Southern way), they often flub the effort. A male friend of mine considered himself a Feminist man. However, he was fond of saying, "I'm the only womanizer who actually likes women". Can you spot the flaw in that reasoning? Feminist men don't become or aspire to be womanizers. Kind of in the same vein as, "Some of my best friends are…"

Another male friend is fond of saying, "If I wasn't married, I would be." (My response is always, "If I was married, I wouldn't be.") He's a great guy, and he thinks of this as a compliment to women, as in, they're indispensable to him. But doesn't that make women kind of interchangeable? I must confess I have never had the nerve to make this argument to him, because he really does seem to have a wonderful wife and an egalitarian marriage, one that I hold up as unique and aspirational, but as I am his friend, not hers, I have only one side of the story, and also, it rankles that if she was gone, it seems he'd just look for another great wife. He's also fond of saying incredulously, "So, if my soulmate was born in China and I never met her, I'd just be out of luck?" He's poking fun at the one-soulmate-for-every-person idea, and possibly reasonably so, but again, it smacks of interchangeability.

Most people don't want to feel interchangeable. I like Willie Nelson, but that song, "To all the Girls I've loved before" is *so* insulting, whether he meant it that way or not. If I was one of those "girls", I'd have to write a rebuttal song called, "Screw you, Willie Nelson, you were nothing special either".

Like women have internalized their inferior roles in society due to millennia of socialization, men also internalized their supposed exalted position, and expect women to take subservient roles and more responsibility in domestic affairs, even as women contribute to the family wealth by working full time outside the home. Some men feel demeaned by doing "women's work". I do believe younger men are doing much better at this, but we are nowhere near full equality of the sexes that can be taken for granted.

Until there is true equality, there cannot be true love. You can mistake passion and/or companionship for it, but without equality, you are just fooling yourself. That's not just my opinion. That's a fact. You do not subordinate someone you love. Keeping someone down is an act of hatred, not love. You cannot think of someone you really love as less than yourself. You do not want less for them than you want for yourself. And you do not get exasperated when they express that this is happening, and wish they'd just go make dinner. Finally, you do not accept sexism and gender injustice as "just the way it is" when it is harming people you truly love.

Men must **not** be allowed to love less than women and call it gender difference. Men must not be allowed to do less family work than women and call it "helping". Men must not be permitted to endorse, enact and benefit from rules that subjugate women and pretend it's fair. Men must not be allowed to satiate their physical drives and call it love. Love is way more than that. Men must not be permitted to reduce love to a contractual transaction (marriage).

Sexism and inequality destroy any possibility of real love. All those seemingly happily married women you know? I've heard them talking. Their love is destroyed even though they don't admit it. But they feel it. They quit loving. They have to talk themselves into still loving their husbands after years, even ***decades of subtle insult and emotional abandonment***. Women know they are not really experiencing love, deep down, because it becomes apparent as they engage in relationships with men, and discuss them with other women. They ignore this abysmal lack of love, or make excuses for it, even blame other women for men's bad behavior. It's all defense mechanisms.

Women pretend they believe in their love relationship, just like humans pretend to believe they have a relationship with pretend Santa god. Perhaps religion and worshipping god is just a socialization technique for getting women to accept one-sided relationships. Women learn that their romantic relationship is like everybody else's, so to want more is eccentric, unrealistic. This is just the way it is, we must accept our disappointment. Work at it, they tell themselves, nothing is perfect. Do you think men are telling themselves that? No, they're telling women that, so that women will lower their expectations and require less effort from men.

The hierarchies created by the masculine way of competition and ranking destroy society. There can be no hierarchies in freedom, happiness and emotional/spiritual fulfillment. Or love. The hierarchy of sexism renders real love impossible. Imagine a world where men hadn't decided to use their larger size and strength to bully others and seize power, but instead had automatically used their size and strength to advance a common, cooperative social effort with emotionally intelligent women as equal partners. Imagine a world where power had not even developed as a concept at all, but people inherently knew to be cooperative instead, with each other and the other Earthlings. ***Imagine there's no power.*** We can't even create a single social system without a power hierarchy, from school boards to clubs to governments. It's a shame. Oh, wait, there is one exception: women are able to have Book Clubs with no hierarchy. That's one. Only one.

What would real, egalitarian love look like? 1)You would always be 100% honest with each other. If one of you asks if they look fat in these jeans, and they do look fat, then the other will answer diplomatically that yes, those are not your best look, they make you look a bit chunky. This way, you will be able to trust what you say to each other and you will not be insulting the other person by assuming they can't handle the truth. 2) **You _must_ be equal in power in the relationship.** 3) You will ***both*** check your egos at the door of your relationship. Consequently, 4) ***both*** of you will put the other's interests before your own. Traditionally, women have often done this, but men have not, resulting in women becoming doormats. No! When your partner is looking out for you, then you are free to spend your energy looking out for them, knowing your interests are covered. When you disagree, you will be arguing from each other's perspective, so there will be no need for anger. 5) You should always make each other feel like the only woman or man in the room, your attention focused on each other above all. Again, women do this more than men and should not. 6) You must believe, know even, that your partner is the best person in the universe. Otherwise, you might keep dating. 7) You must like each other as well as love each other. This is an extremely important point that is often overlooked in the heat of passion. 8) You must make each other laugh every day and perhaps even sing. My aforementioned friend with the egalitarian marriage wrote daily laughter into his actual wedding vows. How great is that? And finally, it's worth stating again because it can't be overstressed, **you must be equal in power in the relationship and must be 100% honest** with each other.

A romantic love relationship can never exist when one party loves the other more than they are loved in return, because then there is an imbalance of power. Any inequality of power cancels out the possibility of real love. A romantic love relationship never feels like settling.

This might sound like a lot of idealized, romanticized nonsense to those who have accepted that love must be a constant compromise. But the fact is we do have an idea of what ideal romantic love is supposed to look like. Look at all the clichés we've come up with for romantic relationships: "two shall become one", love is for "as long as we both shall live", "you complete me", "my other half", or "sex is an expression of love"… They sound really corny because the vast majority of humans can't even come close to achieving them. But it's almost as though we could temporarily see through an opaque veil that normally obscures real love from us, just long enough to pluck the shadow of an idea from behind it about how real love should be (those clichés). For a moment we apprehend it, but it is fleeting, like something told to us in a foreign language we barely know. It's not enough information to be instructive as to how to achieve it, just to write pretty stories about it. And we accept that as the way it must be.

We strive not to be overly starry-eyed and unrealistic about romantic love, but we place no such strictures on ourselves when it comes to god or religion, which actually are ridiculous fantasies and absolutely cannot be realized, no matter how hard we apply our intelligence and efforts. If we held to this standard of love for procreation, as we should, there would definitely NOT be eight fucking billion of us!

Now, let's visit some of our cherished true love clichés:

Sex is an expression of love. That's a good one. Wonder why there is prostitution? Why is sex treated like a basic biological need? Why do men believe they can't go without it? They can go without love.

Two shall become one. Or you're my other half. We practically turn that into a financial and legal contract. The only way in which two become one is by having that joint bank account and not having to testify against each other. Ah, how romantic. Two can't become one because people aren't compatible enough to do so. When you have to pick a needle out of a haystack of 8 BILLION potential partners, your chances of finding someone you're that well matched with, is about 8 BILLION to one. But even if you did, there's still sexism destroying your compatibility.

Love is eternal. Well, divorce. 'Nough said. Sure, real love would be eternal if it could exist, which it can't due to sexism. How many people do you know who are still enthusiastically into each other 20 years after meeting? Even ten years? Too much drudgery and hierarchy.

You complete me. If one person truly completed another person, then when one partner died, the other would spend the rest of their lives incomplete. But almost nobody does that. They wait a respectable amount of time and begin looking for someone new to "complete" them. I've never even found one person who completes me, let alone two! Makes people feel rather interchangeable, doesn't it? And the way things currently are, people are indeed interchangeable. A woman can always find a man willing to put himself above her, and a man can always find a woman who is used to men putting themselves above her and is desperate for a relationship. What a system.

Humans talk a good game about love, (and write a good game, and sing a good game, and sculpt and paint a good game), but they don't actually do it. We are bull shitters when it comes to love, constantly moving the goal posts from ideal to "realistic". And everybody's settling, but especially women. At least men get a servant and that vaunted dick garage out of the deal.

By this point, men must be exhausted from reading about how awful they are. I took a Black Studies course once, and I agreed with and knew most of the stuff they said about white people and racism, but it was still grueling to hear how bad white people are. I kept thinking, "But I'm not like that. Some of us know better." As I went through my life after that, I discovered that some of their complaints did apply to me (the milder ones, like benefitting from white privilege, not realizing how dangerous it was to be Black, and even sometimes seeing skin color before anything else).

So, men, bear with me on this. It's as important to you as it is to women. You are bound by opposite stereotypes and archetypes, but still bound, nonetheless. It must be boring to dress so drably, burdensome to keep your macho guard up at all times, excruciating to suppress your emotions all the time (except apparently when winning or losing the big game), wondering why your partner who used to be so in love with you is cool most of the time. But you're so used to doing it, you don't even notice how fucking difficult it is, like a military man goose stepping through a five mile parade route. You're so well trained in machismo, you do it without thinking. Men should be able to cry. There is nothing quite as cathartic as a good, no-holds-barred bawl. Maybe when Delilah cut Samson's hair, she was doing him a favor, freeing him from having to be strong all the time, allowing him to get in touch with his feminine side.

Women get that great, passionate, tingling love for a few weeks, months or even years, but then it fizzles out and fades away of boredom, drudgery and neglect. But that also happens to men. Nobody wins. Is a dick garage really all you want? All this lack of love leads to women faking orgasms and men faking love. Abolishing sexism and embracing cooperation rather than competition would go a long way toward making real romantic love possible. As things are in this competitive hierarchy, real romantic love cannot and does not exist, and it's a shame that we accept that and content ourselves with just reading it in books and watching shows about it, instead of trying to fix it.

So that thing that we normally call true love that we sense but cannot experience is because brutish, primitive men decided to use their size and strength for power to exploit others, especially women in a pathetic attempt to make themselves feel superior. There were potential alternatives to how we could have evolved. Males could have decided to use their larger size and consequent strength to bring their communities along cooperatively by laboring in support of them and protecting them while recognizing everyone's contribution as equally valuable.

Look, modern men can't help that primitive men created sexism and power based on competition any more than white people can help that primitive white people invented racism, and used it to enslave and abuse people of other groups. But ungrudging acknowledgment and redress would go a long way. I know you don't know this, men, but you'd be happier with love than you are with power. And that dick garage would be a lot more cozy and welcoming.

So, men satisfy women neither sexually nor emotionally, and that has led to the so-called male loneliness epidemic. Men find women's emotional needs exhausting, because they admit none of their own, thus have no experience in handling emotions. Ask a man who complains of loneliness to describe what he means by it, and I'm willing to bet a whole lot of men, especially the ones who blame women for it, would basically describe horniness rather than actual loneliness. They would unlikely describe the problem as wishing they had a woman to have mutually satisfying conversations about topics of interest to both of them with equal give and take. They might really have in mind having a captive audience to whom they can dump their thoughts on subjects of interest to themselves. And then have sex.

Men have been subjected to the same millennia-long socialization as women, just on the opposite side of it. They've been raised to believe they are smarter and stronger than women and should be in charge. And that can serve to mitigate men's culpability for the past sexism they automatically promulgated. But, not anymore. Now, you've been told. Now, you've had it explained to you. You know your sexist behavior is insulting, unwarranted and deleterious. Always! There's no going back to the tired trope of that's just the natural order of things. It isn't. It can change. So, at this point, if you don't learn how to be cooperative with women rather than competitive, you are intentionally being sexist, despite knowing the consequences. So, from here on, that makes you culpable. Guilty!

And one more thing. If men hadn't totally botched sex with sexism, hierarchy, and competition, we might be far more physically evolved to enjoy sex by now. Maybe we would have evolved special muscles in our vaginas and penises which would involuntarily massage just right, when we are aroused, without all that effort and agitation, and sex would be more tranquil, enjoyable, effortless and lengthy. See what you guys did? You stunted our sexual evolution!

***Now, if any men have made it this far through that tirade against you, let me state right now that I actually LOVE men. I think I'm surprisingly far over on the hetero side of the spectrum of sexual orientation. I love the tactile sensations, the looks, the voices, the smells of men. I really do. Wait, am I objectifying men? Did y'all even notice? Physically, you're great. Emotionally, you're a disaster. I just don't like what millennia of sexism have done to you. Y'all need to work on that as urgently as world peace. Cause you unlovable! And women try really hard!

Chapter 5- Is god a Sociopath or a Psychopath?

OK, the title of this chapter was just literary click bait, because this is a very important topic. It doesn't matter whether god is a sociopath or a psychopath, since he does not exist, but humans do exist and one in twenty to twenty-five of us is a sociopath. Fact. We treat sociopathy and psychopathy as this rare, exotic condition, but we have all encountered them in our everyday lives.

Due to the unhappy reality that the U.S. had a sociopath president from 2017 to 2021, a lot had been said about sociopaths then. But the information had been watered down and overly polite. TV personalities kept stating that sociopaths have no empathy, which is true. But it is much more treacherous than that. What nobody could quite bring themselves to report is that sociopaths have no conscience. Perhaps they had a hard time saying this because it makes sociopaths (and donald trump, specifically) seem subhuman and valueless, which maybe they are, they are certainly not quite the same species as normal people. They are definitely humanoid, but I think to be fully human, one must have a conscience.

Since one in 20-25 people are sociopaths with no conscience, chances are you work with at least one. That person who looks your boss square in the eye and lies about what they're accomplishing at work and feels no shame that at least some of you know s/he's lying is your sociopath. That person who passed your idea off as their own is your sociopath. Sociopaths feel no shame, no remorse and possibly cannot be rehabilitated because they lack the basic conscience required to make them feel they need to change.

Sociopaths have a need to control others and have no empathy for those they exploit. The people in their orbit are there to be manipulated, to be used as suckers. They feel this makes them superior. They over value themselves and under value everyone else. They disregard the needs of others and are very critical of anyone who dares to disagree with or challenge them, attempting to destroy any opposition. Other people are pawns to be used for the sociopath's purposes.

They believe the rules don't apply to them. They think they are special and above everyone else. The only time they might express remorse is to get themselves off the hook if they are caught breaking the rules or laws, and even then they will try to claim that everyone else is wrong and they are the only ones who are right and know the truth. (You know, like a witch hunt.) They are skilled at having dupes take the blame for their dishonest activities. Accountability is meaningless to them and they will always do or say whatever is most expedient in the situation. They are dismissive of others and constantly scheme to get their own way.

Sociopaths easily cross over to being psychopaths. Psychopaths are out and out predators. They have criminal minds and are always actively searching for other people to be used as tools to achieve their own ends. They MUST be dominant in all circumstances. They have bad tempers, are abusive and seem to actually enjoy hurting others. Examples of this are donald trump's delight in giving opponents derisive nicknames and bragging about defeating anyone who crossed him, in primary elections, his enjoyment in boasting that he could shoot someone on Fifth Avenue and not be punished. Also, putin's pleasure in murdering his enemies and his relish at imprisoning and torturing them prove his psychopathology.

There are a lot of sociopaths and psychopaths in this world. I did the math. If one in 20-25 people (a conservative estimate) is a sociopath or psychopath, that means of the eight fucking BILLION of us, 320-400 MILLION of us are sociopaths or psychopaths. That's a lot of fucking psychos. We have GOT to become more aware of this issue. I don't understand why this isn't being discussed on every talk show. This is of such astronomical importance! We have got to become aware of this problem so we can protect ourselves. These people are trying to breed with unsuspecting normal people, lying their way into institutions and companies, and worst of all, successfully infiltrating government, by appealing to the grievances of disgruntled populations, namely racist, sexist, straight, white Christian males who are nostalgic for more unwarranted privilege and power.

If we treat this issue as though it's merely a rare aberration, we are missing the point. These fascist sociopaths are running the world. They are fomenting right wing fascist movements all over the globe. They recently arrested a cell of them in Germany, Victor orban is dismantling democracy in Hungary much to the enthusiastic cheering of republicans in America, bolsinaro in Brazil, netanyahu is back in power in Israel, Argentina just fell to a crazy fascist named milei, putin, xi, the nazis just made large electoral gains in Europe, and Africa is just lousy with violent, murderous warlords.

And then there's that beacon of reason and democracy, the United States, daily discovering what abuses of power occurred during our previous fascist regime, that we only escaped temporarily by the skin of our teeth. The sociopath trump gang is back. They are still working at subjugating women and people of color. They have succeeded in repealing women's rights and suppressing voting rights and subverting education. They are relentless and determined. They want their undeserved privilege and power to remain intact and increased, even.

The idea that good will automatically win out over evil is one of those religious platitudes that makes us feel better but simply is not true and can actually be dangerous, by lulling us into a false sense of security and causing us to become lazy and let our guard down. The crazies on the right are armed to the teeth and violent as hell as demonstrated on January 6th. They each possess arsenals that they euphemistically call "collections", and they would be glad to use them. They are not kidding when they say that we'll pry their guns from their cold, dead hands. They are as fond of their guns as they are their dicks. Their guns *are* their dicks. That's how in love with their guns, they are.

The sociopath population is much greater among them, because such a power-mongering movement appeals to them. That means they are willing to do whatever it takes to get their own way. We are in trouble and we are not facing the problem. So few of these domestic terrorists have been jailed, that they are encouraged in their enterprise. These violent sociopaths have threatened elections officials, school board members and government officials and they have done it right out in the open, often on TV and in front of law enforcement and they have not been arrested. We politely escorted them out of the capitol building on January 6th instead of throwing them all in a paddy wagon as would have been done to Black Lives Matter protestors, had they breached the capitol. Their leader trump has enjoyed a leisurely liberty for four years when everyone knows he committed multiple crimes. Where is the deterrence that advocates of punishment endorse so vehemently when it's poor, Black people committing crimes?

These violent psychopaths are encouraged from their lack of accountability, they are emboldened to continue their disgraceful endeavors against the rights of the majority of us normal people. It almost seems as though the white men in power who do nothing to hold them accountable subconsciously support their success. Maybe Mueller and Garland didn't do whatever was necessary to protect democracy because they are privileged, white males who enjoy their power.

Currently, we are in a situation where we need to learn to defend ourselves from sociopaths not only in our private lives, but as a nation and a world community. If we don't understand them, if we can't even believe such terrible humans exist, we can't hold them at bay. If we can't believe that there are people who have virtually no ability to feel kindness for others, we can't prepare ourselves for their schemes. If we can't believe there will never be another Hitler, we can't recognize one when we see him right in front of us.

They are also using the internet wholesale to brainwash and lie to people. There were people who believed that it made no difference who won the U.S. election, because both candidates were awful! They didn't understand that they were literally voting for democracy vs. dictatorship in the 2024 election. They can't even imagine the repressions that are coming with trump as dictator. Russian young people didn't realize it, either, because those born after 1990 had lived their entire lives in a relatively free country, where they could speak their minds. They couldn't imagine that almost overnight, their freedom of speech and democratic institutions could disappear. But it has, and some of them are in prison now or stateless exiles because of it. The same is about to happen in the U.S.

Americans think it can't happen here, but it *is* happening here. And as the U.S. falls to fascism, you can kiss freedom in the whole world goodbye. Because once the U.S. falls, the fascist financers of our downfall will set their sights on the rest of the world, buying elections all over Europe, and there will be no one left to defend democracy, nowhere you can go to be free. I'm not saying the U.S. was perfect and completely free, but our

democracy was certainly the world's best hope. People
of color are not entirely free, women are not completely
free and poor people are not enjoying all the fruits of a
free society, but they were all a hell of a lot better off
than they will be under a trump-imposed, straight, white,
christian, male, theocratic kakistocracy.

Before I learned about the phenomenon of
sociopaths, when I was a young, idealistic person
working in the Criminal Justice System on the Defense
side, I believed everybody could be rehabilitated,
because that was my experience. Most of my clients
were poor, Black people who had been born into grim
circumstances, and some of them had done truly awful
things. But when I talked to them, I did so with dignity
and respect and some clients I got to know very well.
They were often very smart and also had a kind side that
came out when they were treated well. I knew some very
kind murderers and thieves. I would trust any of them
more than I would ever dream of trusting trump. These
were people who were criminals because of their lot in
life. Trump is a criminal because he's greedy, racist,
misogynist and power hungry. And a sociopath, verging
on becoming a psychopath, who enjoys harming people.

Some people can be rehabilitated from a life of
crime. I know this from experience. But you have to
have a conscience to change, because you have to
understand that you're doing wrong, and want to do

better. Trump and putin and many republican politicians don't believe they're wrong. They believe that the only way to live in this world is to take everything you can and leave nothing for others. Anything else makes you a sucker. They don't feel love, only the need to satisfy their needs and sexual urges, but they can temporarily feign love, if necessary to get what they want. They lie as naturally as they breathe.

It is imperative we do not breed with these humanoids, because the trait seems to get passed down through the genes. Sociopaths beget sociopaths. We don't yet know if you can offset genetic sociopathic tendencies with a nurturing environment. But just in case you can't, be very careful who you reproduce with, because as stated previously, you will NOT enjoy raising a little sociopath. For all the time and toil you put into raising them, you will receive virtually no love or caring back from them, although they will feign just enough love that you'll constantly question your judgments of them. Especially be careful about breeding with them, because so far we are the majority, but they breed indiscriminately, feeling no need to take any responsibility for their spawn, and it would be disastrous for them to outnumber normal people.

Most psychologists use the terms sociopath and psychopath interchangeably, however I make a nuanced distinction: sociopaths are willing to do anything, including hurting others, to get what they want; psychopaths seem to actually enjoy having to harm people to get what they want, they enjoy the infliction of pain almost as much as they enjoy getting their own way. It makes them feel even more powerful. Think Vladimir putin. He probably plays the video of Aleksey Navalny screaming out in pain after being poisoned, for fun and recreation.

During the trump administration, newscasters betrayed their basic naivete about sociopathy when they kept asking, when trump would get into trouble, "Do you think he'll resign?" This drove me absolutely nuts, because I knew that he would never resign, never accept defeat, never, ever do anything decent for the sake of the country or his stupid political party, and I would shout at the TV, "NO! Of course he won't resign, it's a stupid question!" They kept acting as though he was a normal human being and he is not. He does not care if he takes the whole party, the whole country, even the whole world down with him. In fact, the greater the scale of damage he could do, the more powerful it would make him feel, and the happier he'd be. He will NEVER, EVER do anything for the good of anyone but himself, EVER. It's important to know what you're dealing with. He is not like you and me. He has no conscience!

These psychos are currently networking on a global scale and trying to form a global, fascist movement to keep women and people of color down. They strategize regularly with other fascist racists and they are making big plans. And again, let me stress that good will not just automatically win out over evil, fascist racism, and if that's our (good people's) strategy, we are going to lose miserably and become subjugated slaves to a global kakistocracy (which is a government by the worst among us). It's really that serious. That's what they want for you and me and your children. They are plotting even as you read this.

You know, tribes have fought each other from the dawn of civilization, but only one race systematically travelled the world, taking possession of every land mass that it could, appropriating all the resources for themselves and enslaving other nations of people. That is the white, European race that did that. Ron DeSantis wants to make sure your children will never learn that even in the watered down way it's taught in school, but it is nevertheless, the truth. The Chinese and Mongols didn't do that when they were at the heights of their power, the Arabs and Ottomans didn't even though they conquered a lot of territory, the Africans and the Indigenous Peoples of the Americas never had an interest in world domination- only the white people, beginning as far back as the Romans, were so greedy as to want to control the whole world.

So, if you think it won't happen again, because we already went through that with the British empire, upon which the sun never set, and we have already eradicated that ghastly injustice, rethink that. The likes of modern fascists like bannon, trump and their foreign allies like putin are quite nostalgic for that era. They consider it not a disgrace, but a badge of honor, a sign of superiority that ruthless Europeans conquered the world through murder and slavery, and they want to return to that circumstance. They are actively plotting for it. So, if you think I sound a little hair-on-fire panicked, you would be right. They are the most heavily armed fanatics in the world and they are literally gunning for us.

So, I guess if there's an answer to the rhetorical question in the title of this chapter, it's that god is a sociopath and a psychopath, because he is them. They are him. He is their mascot, their standard, the banner under which they commit their foul, heinous deeds. God is Tucker Carlson, and I know he'd giggle delightedly like a school girl if he could read this, but it is not meant in the least as a compliment. He and his ilk are pathetic, insecure, miserable, little zeroes, who have nothing to feel good about themselves, so they manufacture the most implausible of accolades for themselves- skin color? Gender? Religion? Miniscule pieces of pink pud that nobody wants? Not accomplishments, but genetics. They know they are gross. Steve bannon knows he is gross. Bernie Sanders and Joe Biden are 1000 times the men they are. And they know it. That's why they're so sad and mad.

It's ironic that the conspiracy theorist trumpster trash nuts who believe that anyone who sees through them is a lizard person in disguise, are basically functioning from the basest part of their brain, what we call the reptilian brain, the brain stem, essentially their lizard brains (with apologies to lizards), which is the part of the brain that simply controls survival instinct (fight or flight), fear, and nothing more sophisticated. But then, they always accuse normal people of committing the offences they are committing.

Republicans have spent the past eight years accusing the Democrat*ic* Party of committing the crimes they themselves were frenziedly committing, such as voter fraud, judicial activism, cheating, lying, stealing, nepotism, all things republicans do as a matter of course. So, not surprisingly, the reptile-brains accuse everyone else of being lizards. They are the ones who, like reptiles, use their brains only to compete to survive. They cannot process the sophisticated concepts of altruism, selflessness and equality, which are recognized even by the foolishly superstitious (the religious) as the bulwarks of true humanity and spirituality.

They are also ***NOT*** patriots, despite their regular flag molestation (Nan, 2023). They do not love the U.S. for its globally respected democratic institutions, because they are willing to dismantle them in order to maintain straight, white, christian, male rule. They only love the U.S. as long as it looks exactly like they want it to look, like a man who trades in a beautiful woman when she begins to lose her looks. They do not get to claim patriotism for themselves. What they are is chauvinists, people committed to feeling superior to others- chauvinists, not patriots. Words matter.

It is imperative that we learn to identify and consequently constrain socio/psychopaths from gaining any positions of power in government and organizations. They are destroyers. This should be a prevalent topic in psychology and even neuroscience research study- it is imperative that we normalize, and even prioritize discussion of this phenomenon, and research how to identify and constrain socio- and psychopaths. Of course, we should include discovering whether or not they are rehabilitatable, salvageable humanoids, and if so, how to do it. But no matter the answer to that, they must be kept from positions of power. And right now global leadership is lousy with these psychos. They've already gotten control of the U.S.

How did the world come to contain all these nazis, fundamentalists, Z people, tribalists, nationalists, patriotic and religious zealots? Just for fun, let's blame the Bible. Because if humanity started with two original humans, say Eve and Adam, then there was a boat load of gene-pool-polluting incest going on. Like, more than the royal families of Europe! To go from two people to 8 fucking billion took an insane amount of incest, and we're not talking distant cousins, we're talking immediate family. This might explain why some men feel free to rape their daughters.

The great movie "Idiocracy" explains present and future morons. It shows a really dumb football player with his arms around as many dumb cheerleaders as he can fit, and he yells, "I'm gonna fuck all y'all!" and then they show a little family tree chart of his numerous genetically dumb offspring. In the next scene, we see an educated, intelligent, thoughtful couple agonizing over every small detail of their plan to have a child until they actually pass the age of their fertility and fail to reproduce.

But how did we get to all these dumb trumpster trash, Z people and assorted tribalist zealots of this current age? You have to go back to say, at least Medieval times to account for it, when the dumbest, most uncouth, least decent men were knocking up the least fortunate prostitutes left and right, leaving their genetic offspring abandoned, desperate and hateful. Those forsaken children were the antecedents of the trumpster and Z trash. The patriarchy makes sure it always has a steady supply of mouth-breathing, knuckle-dragging foot soldiers to protect it.

To reiterate how to spot a socio or psychopath: first, understand that they are not just a rare anomaly, they are everywhere. They will lie about anything to anyone to get what they want. If you catch them in a lie, they will attempt to lie their way out of it. They will never genuinely feel or express remorse for hurting someone, although they might fake contrition to keep a con going. They will never admit they were wrong and never own up to making a mistake. They will certainly never apologize, but if they did something akin to admitting to being wrong it would be a brief, perfunctory, insincere, half-hearted concession, followed by a declaration that it was someone else's fault and they were actually right, and it would only happen if they needed to do it to get themselves out of being held accountable. Remember trump's post-January-6 speech?

They brag about everything and their boasts are often lies. They routinely and casually commit acts of injustice against others. They think of all other humans as a means to their own ends. People who are not as ruthless as them are inferiors to be used as suckers and marks. They treat people who are subordinate to them poorly and disrespectfully, giving them demeaning nicknames and speaking derisively to and about them. If crossed in any way, even over something trivial, they will strike out like a startled snake and try to categorically extinguish any challenger.

They value ruthlessness, competitiveness, and winning. They disdain kindness, charity, cooperation and loss, and have contempt for people who display these characteristics, believing them to be weak, and thus deserving exploitation.

You may not be able to observe all these behaviors in an acquaintance in a timely fashion, so basically, if you find someone being dishonest, unkind and uncaring, observe them carefully over time and do not give them your trust. **Do not engage** with them except in the most perfunctory ways if you must, and be very cautious about what you say to them. They will literally exploit any information you give them about yourself. Stay as far away from a potential sociopath as you possibly can. If possible, safely and confidentially discuss their behaviors with trustworthy others to gather additional information and anecdotes to assess their sociopathy.

Do not try to befriend, engage, or attempt to get justice from these humanoids. They will do whatever it takes to beat you, and you are probably not as pugnacious, intransigent and implacable as they are, so you will spend all your time on a hopeless battle that

they are actually enjoying, but is just sucking your
energy from you. And the worst part is, they will most
likely win and quite possibly cause you harm. They are
not worth the trouble until their kind is understood and
methods are in place to deal with them. Right now, you
cannot go to your boss and say, "Johnson is a sociopath
and we have to keep him from committing injustices."
Your boss won't know what you're talking about and
will think you're being unkind and judgmental. Again,
proving the pressing need to bring this issue to the
forefront. And if you take evidence of unjust behaviors
to your boss, the sociopath will just lie his way out of it
and turn the tables on you.

These are not normal humans. But unfortunately,
they do exist. 325-400 fucking million of them. And they
want no less than to rule the world.

Chapter 6- Fun With Death or Fifty Fun Afterlives for you to obsess over if I've taught you nothing, or hopefully just have fun fantasizing about- a little levity after that morose last chapter

First of all, and I would think this would be obvious, but no bad people allowed. Now, lest you think this system is as harsh as the Christian Heaven-Hell dichotomy, let me assure you that we here at the Fun Afterlife High Commission have made provisions for the rehabilitation of dumbasses. It's called reincarnation. You have to keep going back to Earth until you get it right. Sometimes you have to go as far back as an urban cockroach to start again, (trump and putin may have to literally go back to pond scum), but if you're a narcissistic, sociopathic, or psychopathic subhuman humanoid too many times, you will eventually literally turn to dust when you die. Fair warning putin and trump, Psychopath Boys, those thousands of people you let die of covid and warfare did not help your case. You are very close to being a puff of dust. (If only!)

Fun Afterlife Numero Uno: Perfect Soulmate World - **<u>Soulmatopia</u>**

In this Fun Afterlife, everyone arrives and immediately meets their soulmate, their perfect match. The one person whose appearance takes your breath away, whose every utterance seems like a pearl of wisdom to you, whose jokes all send you into fits of laughter. Likewise, the same holds true for them, your looks send them reeling, they hang on your every word and delight in all of your witticisms. This person smells good, tastes good, sounds and looks beautiful, feels dreamy to touch, they fill up your senses, they are your garden of Earthly delights. And you are the same to them.

Now, for that approximately .000000001% who were lucky enough to have found that person in your lifetime, you can stay together and without all the drudgeries of Earth life, such as child-rearing, work, making a living, money issues, bad smells, illness and exhaustion, your lives will finally be perfect together. Good for you, your reward is freedom, rest and relaxation. I have never met any of you, with the possible exception of Danise, who invented the couple name (short for Dan and Denise) in the 70's, long before there was Bennifer, so please come and introduce yourselves to me when I get there. I am impressed. (Side note: I recently googled Danise and found out Dan is married to someone else now, so there go my only nominees. I have one other that's a possibility, Maurry, so I'm still hopeful.)

But if you are among the phonies who are pretending, just to keep up appearances, woe to you, because the afterlife will sort you out! So, pay attention, especially men, because as surely as women can fake orgasms, they can fake love, and you may get to the afterlife and find out she was just placating your toxically macho ass to keep her life peaceful (when she should have left you and gone out on her own).

You will be able to dance perfectly with your soulmate, never a missed step, and you can sing with them without a sour note, and of course, the sex is perfect every time. (Which means, and I really shouldn't have to say this, but everyone has orgasms.)

Everyone in this fun afterlife gets to revert to their peak age. You won't be shallow and go for optimal physical excellence when you choose, but also take into consideration your emotional and intellectual level. Of course, shallow people wouldn't even be able to attain this fun afterlife, they'd have to wait in some kind of purgatorial afterlife or even reincarnate for further improvement. Wait, you can revert to peak physical appearance (oh, let's be allowed to be a wee bit shallow), but you'll also be at your peak of wisdom. That's better. Makin' it up as I go along.

When you get to this Soulmatopia, you will experience Love At First Sight, only this LAFS will work out in the long term, because instead of getting stale as time passes, it will only get better. The more you get to know each other, the more time you spend together, the more you'll like and love each other. You won't have to work at it. You will never say annoying things to each other, in fact, you are incapable of irritating each other. Neither of you will ever feel like sex when the other doesn't, you will always feel like taking walks at the same time, going dancing, having a drink or a meal, watching a movie or just sitting together, reading. You will be in synch all the time.

You will have the same interests, so if your soulmate feels like doing some gardening, so will you. You will have the same taste in music, shows and décor. Each morning you will both wake up refreshed at the same time and feel like doing the same thing together. If you need some alone time, so will your soulmate at exactly the same time. Or you might just have alone time by reading silently together or basking quietly in sunshine in a double lawn chair.

Each time you see each other, you gaze lovingly at each other and have an overwhelming feeling of love. You both constantly think how lucky you are to have this wonderful person with you. And you never have to worry about losing them, because this is eternity and you cannot lose each other. Neither will ever fall out of love with the other. And it will never get boring. You will forever delight and entertain each other with your compatible perspectives, conversation, and activities as though you are newly in love.

Every time you see their face or hear their voice or touch their body, it will thrill you. You will never tire of each other's face, touch or smell (they will smell good, there are no bad smells in the afterlife! Obviously, there are no warts, eczema, skin tags, whiney voices or other such god-designed Earthly irritants).

A soulmate relationship can never exist when one party loves the other more than they are loved in return, because then there is an imbalance of power. Any inequality of power cancels out the possibility of being soulmates. You and your soulmate will truly live happily ever after, with no documents and religious rituals necessary, just two perfectly matched souls. A soulmate relationship never feels like settling. No one should ever settle- it has to be the least romantic state in the universe. Better to remain single.

Which brings us to Fun Afterlife Number Two: Perfectly Single World - **<u>Singletopia</u>**

In this Fun Afterlife, you are completely happy being alone. You have your own place, your own transportation, your own friends, your own stuff, your own family members who do not live with you, everything is yours, and everything is done your way. You do not ever have to compromise with anyone about anything. You can do whatever you want, whenever you want, why ever you want, wherever you want, whoever you want, however you want, with but one caveat- you may not hurt others (obviously).

Your place is decorated exactly as you like, with no compromise for the taste of another. Your décor can be as masculine or as feminine as you like. If you're a woman and want frilly furniture and accessories, you don't have to worry about emasculating a man. My bedroom is so unapologetically feminine that it could shrivel a straight man's nuts. When I purchased this fabulous furniture, I detected a smidgen of envy from the saleswoman who clearly had a husband whose machismo she had to take into account.

You never feel lonely, even though you are frequently alone. Loneliness doesn't really exist- it's a human construct, much like true love and soulmates, that was created to keep people procreating, an evolutionarily convenient myth that helps preserve the human species. In the afterlife, there is no need for it and it ceases to exist. Loneliness has been crammed down our throats in the Earthly life.

In some languages, like Russian, they don't even have two different words to express the concepts of lonely vs. alone. It's the same word for both- odna. Can you imagine? I am alone most of the time. I am never lonely. So, in this Fun Afterlife, you are comfortable and happy with your own company. You like yourself and you can occupy your time and entertain yourself. You don't always have to be busy, but you can be, if you want. Everything is up to you, and only you. You are immortal and free. Most people in their Earthly life bartered away their freedom for a mediocre relationship which made them feel safe. It's a very poor bargain. (I remind you of the Ben Franklin quote.)

Now, don't get me wrong. In this Fun Afterlife, you don't have to be alone all the time, you can be with other people when you want to be. You can go out with or visit other singles, couples, or groups and you never feel like a fifth wheel, because there is no need for that stupid human construct. You are simply being with people whose company you enjoy. And what's wrong with a fifth wheel- it can be very balancing.

You might even date if you want to, but you both have your own homes. You can stay over at each other's place when you feel like it and then go home when you want to. Your friends and family from your Earthly life might be among those with whom you spend time, and if so, you get along. That crazy trumpster trash uncle who ruined all your Thanksgivings, you don't have to bother with, and you don't feel guilty.

At Christmas, you can decorate as elaborately (or sparsely, if you're a humbug) as you want without someone else in the household exclaiming that it's a little over the top (or too Spartan, if you're a humbug). You can go all Hallmark movie madness on your place and you can keep the decorations up until Easter if you want to (or get that tree down on New Year's Day, if you're a total Scrooge!)

You cook when you want and not one meal more. No one but you ever asks what's for dinner. You aren't responsible for anyone's nutrition but your own. You can have peanut butter and jelly sandwiches for dinner five nights in a row if you want to. Oh, yeah, there's food in the afterlife, just like there's sex. There's drink and drugs, too, and everyone can indulge without being addicted. It's all just recreational and fun- that's why it's called a Fun Afterlife!

Fun Afterlife Number Three: Fun Travel World - **Traveltopia**

You have the ability to materialize anywhere and anytime you want. You don't have to deal with crowded airports, cancellations, rowdy passengers or tiny seats.

Not only can you travel geographically but you can time travel as well. You can go lurk invisibly around that ex-lover you had, back at the time when you were together and learn what the hell they were thinking, because they sure didn't communicate it to you. Ooh, there could be a dead lover lurking around you right now!

You could spend three weeks at the beach, then a month in Venice (before they turned it into a giant shopping mall), a few weeks in Paris, then stroll through Red Square in Moscow during Christmas time before putin's war, take a long leisurely tour of the English countryside on the public right-of-ways, hike around the perimeter of Ireland, smoke a little pot in Amsterdam, anything you wanted. You would have your own ideas-maybe the mountains rather than the beach, Africa, Asia or South America rather than Europe.

Or you could hover over hitler in his bunker in the last day to see if he really killed himself, or more in keeping with his psychopathic personality, killed a double and escaped to Argentina. But, of course you couldn't change anything. All it's good for is learning the truth and satisfying curiosity. We can't have a bunch of time tourist ghosts changing history constantly. How would school children pass their history course if it kept changing constantly?

I would materialize on the grassy knoll in Dallas on the afternoon of November 22, 1963. I already know who did it- I just want to confirm all the players. You could appear visually, too if you preferred, but again not change anything. Civil war fanatics could materialize in a Civil War uniform and participate in a battle. There would be no danger because you're already dead. It would just be a cool experience to satisfy your obsession.

You could join a labor strike or a suffragette demonstration, attend the Stonewall riot, or go to a speakeasy in period attire to blend in. You could attend the first Kentucky Derby or Wimbledon, go to a royal wedding or haunt some evil bastard like trump or putin. You could go ice skating at Rockefeller Center in the 70's with the cast of Saturday Night Live after the Christmas show, or skate the canals of St. Petersburg in tsarist Russia or the canals of Venice during Carnivale, or the canals of Amsterdam as a school child on a field trip.

You could be the ultimate Dead Head and attend every concert, go to Woodstock, or sit in on a jam session of famous musicians at Sting's Tuscan villa, or party at George Clooney's Lake Como mansion, or be on the roof top for the last Beatles concert, or defect from the Soviet Union with Mikhail Barishnikov- how thrilling would that be? You could do things that would make your Earthly bucket list seem trivial by comparison.

You could spend a leisurely, endless, eternal summer touring the world's beaches, or see what the rings of Saturn are like (apparently just gas, but maybe visually interesting), or that big red spot on Jupiter (apparently just a humongous storm), or visit another universe, see if there was any life elsewhere and if it could communicate and was interesting, or are they stupid, filthy animals like so many human Earthlings.

You could spend some time at Kurt Vonnegut's place to see if he was as funny and fascinating as his books, but you would have to be invisible because any celebrity is likely to have you thrown out for trespassing, as well they should. There is no right to intrude on famous people. You could sit unseen, on the couch of a late night talk show and pretend you were the guest and answer all the questions the host asked as if they were for you. But for god's sake, try to be witty and don't presume anyone cares about your professional process! Viewers just want to be entertained at the end of a long day. If you don't have a shit ton of hilarious stories `a la Tom Hanks, just stay home. I don't care how much flesh you flash, it doesn't make up for being boring. I may be getting a bit grumpy here, time to move on.

Notice there are no references here to Beyonce', Billie Eilish, Taylor Swift, hip hop stars, so-called reality show "celebrities", or so-called "influencers". That's because I'm around 70 and I don't care about that stuff. The whole point is that you make up your own fantasy materializations and time travel trips. I'm just throwing out examples but everyone has their own interests and fantasies. I can't read your mind. Use your imagination. I can't do everything! At this point, I get frustrated because half the time I've never heard of the guest hosts on Saturday Night Live anymore, and I almost never recognize the musical guests, so, OK, Millenials, (said like they say "OK, Boomer") Gen X, Y, and Z, use your imagination, go where you want to go, but hopefully you won't be dying too soon.

By the way, a word about the above younger generations; I don't feel snarky about them, I appreciate them for bringing veganism into the mainstream, even though they pronounce it weirdly. It should be pronounced vejun with a short e, because it's derived from vegetables, but that's OK, at least they made it widespread enough that it's profitable for companies to come up with veggie entrees that don't taste like sawdust, so I thank you guys. Also, most of you aren't as racist, sexist and homophobic as the generations before you, so good for you. Keep voting and get rid of these sexist, racist, homophobic, old white males in charge, and you might end up in a pretty decent world. You give me hope in a dark time when a minority of sick ass, little-dicked, pathetically insecure nazis are trying to take over. Oops, getting cranky again, better move on.

Maybe it was nice people enjoying a Fun Afterlife who put those stainless steel pillars all over the world and then took them down just as mysteriously. (I actually think that mystery has been resolved but I forget how, so it's just fun to think about it.) Maybe Fun Afterlifers erected that statue of Melania trump's ugly soul in her home country of Slovenia and then burnt it in effigy as a warning to racist, autocratic people of what happens to shitheads in the Un-Fun Afterlife of HELL!

Long story short (too late), this is the Fun Afterlife where you can tick off a bucket list the length of eternity. No time limits, just endless opportunity and freedom to do whatever you want, go wherever you want, satisfy all your aspirations, whims and curiosities. Where would you go?

Fun Afterlife Number Four: Fun Super Power World- **<u>Superpowertopia</u>**

You can go back to Earth or anywhere you want and you are invisible and you can fly and see through all pretensions and understand people's true characters. I call this particular super power being able to see through people's clothes, but not just what they're spanxing up, you can see what they really think and feel, who they really are.

How would this be useful or enjoyable? Well, right off the bat and most obviously, flying is just sensational. You might not even care about the other two super powers once you got a taste of out-of-body flight. You can't bring your big old bulky body, that's just Physics, so you just bring your essence. Many people have done this in dreams and it feels exquisite. In this Fun Afterlife, you will have complete control over when, where, and how you'll fly. Flying in my dreams is the only phenomenon that ever gave me even the slightest hint that there could be something like a soul that can survive to enjoy a Fun Afterlife. (Don't ruin this for me, Physicists and Neuroscientists by explaining to me how it is no such evidence- just let me have this nice fantasy while I'm writing this for the nice people. We'll come back to this later.)

How might seeing through people's facades be interesting or enjoyable? You could go back and examine all the terrible people you've encountered, from drunk uncles to toxic co-workers and find out why they are the way they are. 24 times out of 25, it's just some sort of insecurity resulting from bad experiences they couldn't reconcile. The 25th is that sociopath, so who cares about them? They're going back to Earth as a cockroach.

Maybe you'd like the super power of being able to talk to or communicate with animals. I'd love that. Boy, I'll bet they think we're assholes. They're probably thinking, "How many more millennia is it going to take for these morons to rectify the food chain and quit mass murdering us?" We really must quit cannibalizing our fellow Earthlings. I'd like to hear about animals' emotions and their thoughts on the meaning of life. They might realize it's really just survival, reproduction and that's all. They may have some superior wisdom, you never know, because we can't communicate with them very deeply. I hope they're not superstitious, like humans. That would be very disappointing. I don't think they're that dumb.

I guess you can choose your own super power, but if you're just going to copy some Marvel comics power, like spinning webs or turning into an ant or whatever dumb things they do, you're probably not advanced enough for the Fun Afterlife experience. The idea of super heroes is itself childish and clinging to the savior idea, which we need to get past. I recently learned of a theory on the Big Think on You Tube (can't remember the presenter, but it was about why humans allow sociopaths to have power) that humans are evolutionarily predisposed to turn to a strong man in times of trouble, which are, let's face it, always. This goes back to cave man days, when everyone turned to the strongest man in the clan to protect them, so it's ingrained to still turn to a strongman when we feel threatened. We really need to evolve more. That's why trump attracted so many evolutionarily-challenged (I'm being so polite, so politically correct) *humanoids* to his little aspiring dictatorship. He talks tough. But I'd like to see what would happen if we threw him in a pit with putin and sent down only one meal a day.

Here's a fun super power for you to consider. You could spread happiness and intelligence wherever you went. If you saw someone begging on the street, you could hand them fifty bucks, but you could also sprinkle them with happiness and smartness dust, like Tinkerbell. They would figure out what they needed to do to overcome their issues and live a happier life. I'd like to be able to undo sociopaths. We really do not need them in the world.

How about the super power of figuring out the meaning of life, even if it turns out to be just organisms living and dying and trying to create something in their short life spans that is also someday going to turn to dust. Good to know.

I'd like the superpower of being able to speak every human language ever spoken. Go to Italy, speak Italian, go to Russia, speak Russian. Go to ancient Sumeria, speak Sumerian. That would be a superpower. You could listen in on ancient Greek philosophers holding forth at their lectures. You could listen to Attila the Hun plan his battle strategy (that might be a bit much for a modern sensibility to take, but still, you could if you had the stomach for it). You could converse with ancient Chinese philosophers or watch Hindu priests write the Vedas.

And how cool would it be to be able to follow the trail of language families such as Indo-European, Semitic, African, Eastern Asian, and Indigenous American as they developed, spread and changed? What were people thinking when they got in catamarans and crossed thousands of miles of ocean to unknown islands? Or crossed the theoretical land bridge from Asia to America? People are stupid brave! But they were probably driven by necessity when unevolved, violent, knuckle dragging opponents stole their land.

Comedians have a super power. (Even though many of them are ignorant of vegan food.) The ability to make people laugh is a super power. Laughter is a healthy form of happiness, even if somewhat fleeting. That's a super power to be able to make people happy, even for a short time. I would definitely choose that one.

So, let's see. I have chosen invisibility, flying, seeing through people's pretensions, universal language ability, making people happy, figuring out the meaning of life, and comic genius. What are yours?

Fun Afterlife Number Five: Comic Opera Ballet World- **Talentopia**

In this Fun Afterlife, everyone sings beautifully and their every motion is graceful dance. Now I would sing opera and move like a ballerina whose feet miraculously were not sexistly destroyed by dancing on point. You can sing and dance rock, jazz, hip hop or whatever you want.

Anything you said would come out in a perfect melody, so you would actually be organically writing music every time you had something to say. It would just come naturally, like some composers describe certain songs come to them. But this would be all the time. Your life is accompanied by a constant, beautiful, original score. Basically, your life is one long opera, so that's why I called this *Comic* Opera Ballet world, because if I were you, I'd stay with the comedies. The tragedies are so damned melodramatic, it would be taxing on your psyche, but of course, it's up to you. Someone's always dying of consumption, or killing their brother without realizing they're their brother, or accidentally sleeping with their mother, really bad stuff.

Me, I'm going to flit around on my toes in a beautiful, lace and taffeta, elaborately embroidered tutu, singing my heart out, but you can shake your booty all you want, and the thrill of it will be, we'll never tire out or be out of breath. You walk out to the car, you're dancing. Someone cuts you off at an intersection, you cuss them out exquisitely in song and they respond just as elegantly- you can't even stay mad under those circumstances. You curse each other simultaneously in harmony. You smile at the great music, imagine your persecutor is a hell of a dancer, too and hope to see them again sometime.

Conversations with friends and family are concerts. Whatever idea you're trying to convey will automatically be emitted as a musical score magically matched to your movements of dance. Everyone is witty and there is no such thing as a dull conversation or a clumsy motion. You will be costumed to your own taste, which can be elaborate, like a stage production or simple like normal life. You can choose tutus, elegant gowns, period clothes or comfortable garb. If fashion is your art form, go to town. If not, don't worry about it, you're going to look good anyway, because the costumes manifest the same way as the music and fit the occasion.

Your life has major Metropolitan Opera production values.

Fun Afterlife Number Six: Screening Room World- **MyLifetopia**

Maybe this one's a little self-absorbed, but you get to enjoy perpetual screening of your life and history. You can go back and revisit every birthday, holiday, important occasion or ordinary day in your life. It's like an endless wedding video with every detail, every moment. You can watch random days just to see what was going on, revisit your glory days, or your salad days. Revisit old friendships, old lovers, or see what was going on with you before you established memory as a toddler. Check out your ancestors' lives!

There will be a comprehensive, computerized index of your life and history categorized by places, people, preoccupations, and periods, for easy access on an electronic tablet on your lap. You will be seated in the most comfy recliner, which will also manage to be attractive, a feat apparently not possible in Earth life. (Why the fuck can't they make a pretty recliner???!!! Why do they all have to be bulky and ugly???!!!! You know I'm right about this. I'm getting curmudgeonly again, time to move on.) This lovely recliner will have an accessory/snack tray with a cup holder right where your hand falls, and you will be supplied with a bottomless bucket of hot, vegan-buttered, salty popcorn and a refreshing beverage of choice. Since you're already dead, you won't have to worry about weight gain or hypertension from all the salt. There will be vegan Goobers and Raisinettes or whatever you like, too. A meal isn't a meal without dessert.

Bonus! You can edit as you like. It won't change the past, but you can make your life story more to suit you. To loosely quote Eli Wallach in *The Holiday,* if you were the best friend in your life, you can edit it to be the star in your movie. And you won't have to bother with that cumbersome editing equipment, it will be thought activated editing. Just leave that embarrassing ex on the cutting room floor to be swept away with all the other detritus.

Add whatever soundtrack you want. Use your favorite songs. There are no copyright issues here. In fact, there's even an awards show you can watch each year to see which artist was used in the most soundtracks. Beethoven and Tchaikovsky are still kicking ass at that show after centuries, because *Ode To Joy* and *1812 Overture* are freaking timeless. (And everyone knows them from cereal commercials. Let's be honest.)

Your life will be so polished, so perfect by the time you're finished, you'll want to invite everyone over to view it with you. And it won't be like boring vacation videos, it will be an Oscar quality movie, with a plot, a good story, well-told, with something to say, an important message, like good literature. So, take all the time you need. This is your chance to get your life just right.

Fun Afterlife Number Seven: Holiday All the Time World- **Holidaytopia**

Every day's a holiday. And you get to pick which one or make up your own. It can be Christmas one month, your birthday the next day, Easter, St. Patrick's Day, Arbor Day, International Women's day, May Day, Octoberfest, you get the picture. You can decorate for each holiday just by dreaming up the ornamentation. You know those year-round trees that people decorate for every season? Well, you can decorate yours with your thoughts, for real, not the fake way trump declassified documents with what passes for his "mind". So, there's no labor involved. You can change your elaborate holiday decorations every day if you want, just by thinking what you want. And don't forget the garlands and other bric-a-brac. You can decorate as elaborately for Labor Day and your birthday as you do for Christmas.

You get to decide what the festivities will entail. Will you dance around a maypole, get rowdy with some drinking buddies, have a luxurious meal, exchange gifts, listen to special seasonal music or watch holiday movies? Maybe you'll just drink hot cocoa by a fire or read a book under a shade tree with a cold glass of Riesling. There's no pressure to do anything in particular, however you feel like celebrating.

Each day is special and you can do whatever you want, kind of like retirement, only you still have to do the physical work to clean and decorate for holidays in retirement. You can make up holidays, like World Vegan Day, commemorating the day meat was finally phased out for good, or Turkey Thanks Day, honoring turkeys for not being eaten on Thanksgiving anymore. You could have Dog Day or Friendship Day, Hip Hop Day or Jazz Day, Beach Day or Mountains Day, Ancestors Day, Atheists Day. You could easily think up at least 365 of them, and you don't even need that many because Christmas itself lasts from Halloween to Valentine's Day (Easter at my house). If you love St. Patrick's Day, you could make the whole month of March St. Patrick's Day season and stay decorated and in that special Kiss-me-I'm-Irish mood all month. You could stay hammered all month if you want to, because you're dead and the alcohol can't hurt you anymore. The idea is that you just get to keep that special feeling.

I went to Venice once (before they turned it into a shopping mall, when it was still a real city) when I was still working and when I got back I vowed not to lose that special vacation afterglow when I returned to work. But hard as I tried, my everyday life took over and it had vanished by lunchtime! I had lost the rhythmic rocking sensation that had lingered from the vaporetti and the thrill of the novelty, and I couldn't get it back, even in my free time. That won't happen to you in Holidaytopia. You will be able to maintain those special holiday feelings as long as you want, because there won't be any mundanities to interfere with them. Imagine waking up with holiday excitement every day.

Well, by now it should seem obvious that we're not going to make 50 Fun Afterlives as promised in the chapter title, because I'm running out of steam, but just a brief few more:

Celebritopia: You can be a celebrity in any field you want- music, art, film, theatre, science, literature, philosophy, anything. You just can't be someone else. You can be a science celebrity, like Neil DeGrasse Tyson or Bill Nye, you just can't be them. They are them. You shouldn't want to be someone else anyway; you're probably not evolved enough to be in the Fun

Afterlife if you don't want to be yourself, back to Earth you go. (And notice how much kinder and gentler this system is: you either go back to beautiful, wonderful, sunny, beachy, rainy, foresty Earth for further evolving, or you turn to dust. No punitive Hell!)

You can go on talk shows, give lectures, have a podcast or a TV show. You can be super Beyonce' level famous or just be a minor celebrity with a specialized following and still have a modicum of privacy if you prefer. The point is you'll be appreciated for your work, whatever that may be, your choice.

Artopia: You get to live inside of art, truly experience it, inhabit it. You can enter an 18th century French landscape painting, a Van Gogh, a Chinese ink painting, or an early American wilderness, or see what it's like in an abstract Jackson Pollack or Picasso. Any work of art you want, you can get inside it and live it. You can be the David one day, the Thinker the next, then the Venus de Milo. You can enter the cave paintings at Lascaux or just go look at them, since they are apparently closed to the public, now. You could create your own work of art and do whatever you want with it. Maybe you'd just want to go watch an ancient gilded religious text being created centuries ago by monk scribes.

You could get together with other art travelers and discuss art to your hearts' content. You could have dead artists as guest speakers.

Foodtopia: You can eat anything you want (as long as it's vegan, shut up, them's the rules) and drink whatever you want and you never get fat, you never get stuffed, you never get gassy, which I think goes without saying, you never get uncomfortable in any way. You can eat constantly if you want. You can have an endless feast with all your friends, some interesting strangers, with someone special, or just by yourself.

You could alternate eating and napping. Whatever you were in the mood for would just materialize by thinking it up. You can conjure elegant formal dining with exquisite linens, china and crystal or have a junk food binge on a tray on the sofa while watching TV. Food, glorious food, 24/7. Now, that's a Fun Afterlife!

InfiniteOffspringtopia: You can get to know every possible combo of sperm and egg you ever made or could have made, as though they had been conceived, born and raised, without actually raising the human population, because they are all in your mind. Like, who would have been created if you had conceived the time you had that great sex at the beach, for instance? Or on your birthday? Or even, if you're curious, that time you had the bad sex with the dumbass. Or just a random selection?

You could sit down and have a chatty meal with any prospective offspring you ever could have created and find out what they're like. You could get to know that child you aborted, who would probably understand why you did what you had to do and be OK with it. (After all, they escaped suffering a world full of religious idiots.) You could get to know their personalities without all the drudgery of raising them. (Cue the sanctimonious, protesting that child rearing is NOT drudgery! They're only trying to convince themselves, like religious nuts who feel the need to take every opportunity to preach about god and Jesus.) You can conjure your infinite offspring for a meet, but they don't have to suffer life on this seductive but fatally flawed world. Win, win!

***

Magical thinking is fun, as long as you don't confuse it with the truth, just like magic can be fun if you don't become deluded by illusion. You have to be a grown up. We have to evolve. You can still play; that's what this chapter is about. But you have to live in reality. You can invent an imaginary friend like Jesus if you're lonely or scared or just need a confidante, but when you begin to believe he's giving you orders that everybody else has to follow, too, well, then you're just nuts.

157

Religion is basically collective mental illness, we're just all too polite to say so.

Keep your fantasies to yourself, unless someone invites you to share them. The trouble with religion is that it's too promiscuous. Don't be a religion whore, spreading it all over the place inappropriately. (With apologies to whores, who are more discreet.) Don't be trying to give others your mental disease. Religiosity should be as private as sex. Just like you don't want to see people having orgasms in public, no one wants to see you carrying on about Jesus and god in public. Relegate your religion orgies to the privacy of your own home, temple or church. Don't bring it to work, don't bring it to a stranger's door for chrissake, and do NOT bring it into the political arena. Religious harassment is as bad as sexual harassment and qualitatively the same.

Rhapsodizing about your imaginary friend in public is every bit as embarrassing as masturbating in public. In fact, it's exactly the same thing- your Jesus makes you feel ecstatic. Please don't religiously masturbate in public. Normal people, I'm sure you'll agree, don't masturbate in public. So, pull yourself together! Have some goddamned dignity. Normal people don't want to have to see all that orgiastic hallelujahing, fainting for Jesus, acting like fools, "witnessing" (badgering), shouting in tongues, snake charming, working yourselves into a frenzy and going all freaky for religion. Don't become religiously aroused in public. It's gross and promiscuous.

Chapter 7- Is Death Really that Scary?
And The Beauty of Randomness

As I mentioned, I'm around 70 and I'm not going to be around a whole lot longer. And I'm good with that. I've had a pretty long, happy life and quite frankly, I'm a bit tired. I'm looking forward to eternal rest. I don't fear nonexistence at all, even though I can't quite imagine it because to imagine it, one has to exist. Like my mother before me, I'm not looking forward to the process, since we live in such an evil world where we are all murdered against our will. My murderer will be cancer, unless I accidentally walk out in front of a bus, which as my sister Nan pointed out is pretty unlikely where I am. Or unless some pathetic, religious absurdity of a humanoid shoots me. I don't care.

Apparently, people have a tendency to become more religious as they get older, anecdotal evidence of which, is all the current religious nuts amidst the unbridled, wild crew I grew up with, who vehemently eschewed piety and religion in their youth. They seem to get scared of the great unknown and want to hedge their bets. This is Pascal's wager, which avers that you have nothing to lose by believing in god, because if it turns out not to be true, you would have lost nothing, but you have everything to lose by not believing in god, because if he turns out to exist and really is the punitive bastard we think he is (my words, not Pascal's), you will languish in the torture of eternal Hellfire! My response to that is that it just shows you don't really believe, because if you did, that argument wouldn't make sense, since it would be inconceivable for god to be fooled by a false faith of convenience. You mean if I accept Jesus Christ as my Lord And Savior right before I take my last breath, he won't know I was only hedging my bets? Can I trick Jesus?

Why are people so afraid of death? It's facing the unknown, but actually, so is graduation, marriage, having children, buying a house, moving, starting a new job, and retirement, but people do these things all the time and although they are frightened, they proceed hoping for the best. But when it comes to death, they have to make up an ironclad guarantee of success, they're so terrified. Maybe it's because they have no one who has already experienced it to advise them.

When you graduate, you'll either do well or not, when you marry, you'll either be happy together or you won't, you'll either have joyous kids or not, when you buy a house, you'll either get a good house or a bad one, when you retire, you'll either enjoy life or be bored, but when you die, you won't "go" to either Heaven or Hell; either something will happen or nothing will happen to you. Humans can't accept that fact, because in life, they are used to thinking there is something they can do to affect the outcome. They will work real hard, parent real well, do their research, arrange it so they at least optimize their chances. There is no way to enhance your chances in death. Either you will still exist in some form, or you won't, whether you like that or not. There is no way to hedge your bets. Que sera, sera!

Wernher Von Braun, ex-nazi scientist and religionist claims that science tells us that nothing in nature, not even the tiniest particle, can disappear without a trace. Nature does not know extinction, only transformation, so he thinks this means that after death, humans live on as souls in a spiritual realm. As he was a nazi and a religionist, I don't know how credible that assertion is. Seems to me there's a gap in his reasoning about the size of the Grand Canyon; it's quite the leap from there being a transformation, to concluding that the transformation is to souls. There are other options for what form that transformation might take. Isn't it just as reasonable to assume we just decompose after death and the transformation is that we nourish worms and soil, grow into plants, which get eaten by animals and we're in an endless, exhausting cycle of material existence that tires me out just to think about it. Wernher's souls might just turn out to be Wernher's worms!

I don't want to be part of a tree standing for years in the wind and rain and snow, even in exchange for the idyllic moments in the sun. I want *not* to be on the Earth. I'm tired! But there is virtually nothing I can do to ensure that outcome. It does suck not having control of one's destiny- that's one of the reasons scared men invented religion, to pretend that they do.

Lovely as it's been, Earth is a kind of uncannily camouflaged hell that is so alluringly beautiful, that it appears to be Heaven at times and so, few ever want to leave it. Indeed, only 1-2% of humans willingly do so via suicide, and let's face it, they're almost always suffering in some way when they do. The hellishness of this world, the scarcity of resources, lack of love, the diseases, accidents, war, hatred, etc. is offset by the sheer beauty of the place, the beaches, forests, sunshine, cuisine, senses, emotions, etc…

Who would ever stop or stay on this puny, little planet if it wasn't so cunningly marketed? Like one of those perfectly restored, little French medieval villages for the tourists, they're breathtakingly charming, but far from authentic medieval villages, they are essentially cute, over-priced shopping malls with artist colonies attached, which nothing wrong with that, just don't believe you're experiencing a medieval French village when what you're experiencing is a tourist trap. The exquisiteness is Earth's hook. But we're disguising a faulty product, the above-named hellishness.

I suffer from a disease I made up myself called Worst Case Scenario Syndrome or WCSS, where in every situation, my mind automatically goes to the worst thing that could happen. If I have to have surgery, I go right to I could die, which is obviously true even if unlikely. And that's because our little Hell-heaven planet is the Worst Case Scenario world, what with all the disease, disaster, the food chain, accidents, violence, oppression, and competition. Therefore, the shocking horror that occurs here would be the most pronounced characteristic of this planet, if you saw it suddenly for the first time and hadn't been gradually inured to its depravities as we all have been. This fact drives my mind in every situation right to the worst case scenario, as though I have PTSD from being on Earth.

Talk about a worst case scenario world! Men hate women and claim to love them, humans hate and abuse all the other animals, earthquakes, floods, famine! No decent, self-respecting world tolerates these things! Putins, hitlers, trumps… and we think it's all normal, natural and inevitable! Dear fucking Jesus, how can we NOT have permanently defeated this small (but growing) minority of insecure, sociopathic destroyers, spoilers and ruiners, by now? Likewise, how could the rich and powerful 1% keep the 99% down throughout history? Our world is cringey as hell. It's a downright embarrassment! I wouldn't admit I was from here if I went to another planet. Like traveling abroad when there's a republican president, you're just so embarrassed and apologetic.

The world is such a bewildering combination of beautiful and attractive, plus ugly and repellent. The ocean is amazingly spectacular, but then there's horrendous war and violence. The food is fantastic, but flatulence and feces is frightful. Music and Art are so delightful, but then there's traffic noise, tenements and commie blocks. The Earth is like a beautiful person who turns out to have a very unstable personality.

Anyway, at the end of my life, I still chuckle at Pascal's little wager. I am not one tiny iota concerned. There *are* Atheists in foxholes. My wonderful, intelligent, born-Feminist Mother was one. And I am, too. I am sorry for the world I am leaving behind- I did try in my own small, ineffectual way to help improve things a bit, but now I'm just too tired. I fear the entire world is about to go through a fascist movement of white male backlash (to being only equal to everyone else, instead of having privilege that gives them all the advantages) before we can get on with things. I hope we can extinguish it before it destroys humanity and the planet, or even just causes trouble, like WW3 or a 500 year Dark Ages. And again, I remind these small-penised, insecure, pathetic white males who clearly don't believe they can compete on a level playing field where everyone has an equal chance, if you get too cruel, it just might piss people off enough to turn on you as savagely as you are trying to treat them. Be careful how much you piss people off. By trying to preserve white privilege, you just might get the white race wiped off the planet. Right now, everyone just wants equality, but you keep fucking with them.

***

Moving on. A few more random thoughts. First, on randomness. People are so afraid of randomness. It is, for some reason, so unappealing to them that they had to invent Santa god to try to make it go away. But you cannot impose order on a random universe by inventing myths. The thing is, randomness is far better than anything humanity has come up with, because it made each and every one of us a miracle (some more miraculous than others, trumpster and Z trash). Out of the millions of eggs your Mom produced, the one, single, solitary, particular egg that could make you just happened to be randomly fertilized by the one, single solitary, particular sperm of the billions produced by your biological father that would create you. No two other eggs and sperm would have created you. They would have made someone else entirely, like a sibling. That's an amazing miracle. And it was completely random.

166

It depended on so many arbitrary variables, like where your Mom was in her cycle when your egg dropped, if and when your parents decided to have sex, and internal conditions pertaining to incubation. We are all completely random, amazing miracles. Think of it. If your parents had decided to put sex off until the following day, conditions may have changed, and someone besides you may have been conceived. There is nothing mystical about each being's miraculousness, it's a fact of nature, namely biology. (This is not my original thought. I read it somewhere, but I have no idea where, so unfortunately I cannot attribute it. But please claim it, if it is yours, and I will add a citation.)

Why can we not embrace randomness? It is the essence of us. We don't need a god. Randomness is miracle enough. Our individual existence is miracle enough. Why do we reject the truly miraculous creation of ourselves? The random accident that out of trillions of possible combinations of genes, the one that made it to existence is ours? We should revel in that. We should be grateful that randomness has given us this opportunity to experience existence and do our best with it in kindness. Because that's most likely all there is. But it's enough. It's plenty. Actually, it's more than we ingrates deserve, making up silly fairy tales to explain away the sheer exquisiteness of our one in quintrillions chance at existence. We get to breathe air, taste food, feel warmth, and see beauty. And if we're lucky, careful, and energetic enough, we maybe get to do some self actualizing and leave a little something behind for future generations (as opposed to just leaving behind future generations).

All of this awe-inspiring uniqueness and what does humanity do with it? They seek sameness. Like the idea of all merging together into the godhead thingy in some traditions. Eww! To be just a minor cell in a glob. To be one of Jesus' millions of human concubines after death. Why would anyone aspire to that? To be like everybody else in life, and strive not to stick out too much, even to one's own detriment, by observing society's sacred cows, such as patriotism, religionism, sexism, hierarchy, competition and all the rest of the masculinist inventions that allot power.

When I was young, I thought I could (and fully expected to) change the world for the better. I figured all you had to do was show people what was right. I didn't realize how entrenched people are in their beliefs, because their beliefs define their identity. Most humans think that changing their beliefs is tantamount to death. It isn't, but it's in the interests of the church, state, cult leaders and specieists to convince them it is. I have changed my identity a few times. I was a christian who became an Atheist. I was a patriot who became a philosophical anarchist and a critic of my country's ways. I was an apex predator who became a vegan. It's hard to change your identity because it takes thought and planning. But it doesn't kill you.

The absolute worst thing we can do with our randomness-given existence is to use it to stifle others' experience of their miraculous existence by cheating, harming, or using them (this, of course, includes the other animals). People who exploit others and don't share should be shunned, because they are using others' miraculous existence to merely materially enhance their own pathetic life. Any low life bottom feeder can get ahead by using others, but evolved beings at least try to take others along with them. That takes intelligence and kindness, the most evolved traits of all.

We are all smarter than god. I know that I am smarter than god. I hope that I have contributed to demonstrating that you are, too, you crazy, wonderful, random miracle. Dogs and llamas and even lizards and roses are smarter than god, too.

***

The first time I heard the faddish new theory that humans are genetically wired for religion, I thought, "Balderdash!" What we are is genetically predisposed to abhor uncertainty. Ambiguity makes us feel like we may be unsafe, because we cannot control what we don't know. Not being safe makes us afraid, so we make stuff

169

up to explain the unknown and make ourselves feel better. That's your genetic code for religiosity- it's just garden variety fear of the unknown. We are genetically coded for fear, because that helped us to survive back in our primitive origins.

As we observed the fate of other living beings, we realized that our own fate could well turn out to be unpleasant. That made us fearful. So, we endeavored to mitigate our fate, hoping to appease it and make it go our way. We invented rules and developed paths, rituals, and behaviors to get on Fate's good side. Fate became personified as god. And while he was a tough god so that he could protect us, he was also a sugar daddy god, as long as we behaved as he dictated. And tithed. And that's religion in a nutshell, nothing mystical about it.

The human mind abhors a knowledge vacuum, so it rushes to fill it with the easiest, quickest solution it can conjure, which is magic. Religion is mostly magic, with some historical sounding stuff thrown in to make it seem credible.

The three elements of most religions are:

1) Teachings, or the foundational story or myth, which is the historical sounding stuff, and it's actually permissible to borrow it from a previous tradition to give it more plausibility, like Christianity and Buddhism did. This also includes the basic beliefs and tenets;

2) Commentary, which includes important exegesis, polemics, findings, and accepted amendments, that are included in the religious traditions, such as the Hadith in Islam and the Talmud in Judaism; and

3) Rules, last but by no means least, the method by which you achieve the security you're seeking. And the aspect that bestows power on a select few- the rules police- priests, popes and politicians.

Most, if not all religions have these, including Buddhism and Hinduism.

Then there are people who recognize religion for the balderdash that it is and try to find the real truth. They are scientists and philosophers who engage in original thinking and perform experiments. They start with an educated observational guess and then test and re-test their guess until they can determine whether their guess is right or wrong. True, we are loath to let go of our guesses when they turn out to be wrong, but we must in order to distinguish our efforts from dogma.

Every time a theory is confirmed which proves some magical tenet to be dubious, it threatens somebody's power that is based on that magical doctrine. If people were persuaded of a disproof of religious canon, what would occur? The Earth wouldn't be destroyed because there is no god to do so. Nobody would die over it for the same reason, plus clearly religion hasn't been preventing people from dying. Evil wouldn't overtake the Earth because religion isn't keeping it at bay. Humans are being evil anyway, (trump, putin, hitler, netanyahu, etc.) so what would be the consequences of people abandoning god? Only one thing- loss of power for the keepers of the rules.

It's mighty important to the powerful to offer a plausible response to any threat to religious doctrine and authority, such as the Problem of Evil. Since Saul the Jew became Paul the Christian on the road to Damascus (wasn't that a Bob Hope movie?) and turned Yahweh into a lover, not a fighter, the Problem of Evil has dogged religious doctrine (until it was resolved above with the Food Chain Error Fix).

There's only one rule that matters. Every religion professes it but then proceeds to break it, but if every person followed it, there would be zero need for any of the rest of religion- the parts that provide wardens for obscure behaviors, the ones that give those wardens (priests, kings, etc) their power. You know what that rule is: Treat others the way you want to be treated.

The Problem of Evil (POE) drives theologians insane, because deep down, they know religion is a fraud. They are well read, educated people, who like everyone else, also have a gut instinct that Santa god cannot be real. And if religion is a fraud, they know that they themselves, their entire life's work, their identities are a fraud.

They understand that the POE is a metaphorical church door that's cracked open, though it's supposed to be closed and locked to contain humanity inside. That crack allows anyone who sees it to simply push it open and free themselves and possibly everyone else. So, they try to distract the parishioners from the bright sunlight shining through that crack, redirect attention away from the blaring light that signals freedom from superstitious bondage, like a magician performing an illusion: "What beam of light? There's no sunshine coming through that crack! That's not sunlight! It's the fires of Hell! That's Satan luring you! Look over here at Jesus on the cross saving you!"

The ancient Hebrews didn't have quite this version of the problem. They had simply invented a vengeful, terror-wreaking, protector god who looked out for his own. The Jews' only Problem of Evil was why does our supremely powerful god let bad things happen to us? Like, over and over and over. They can and do easily reason that their angry, vengeful god was just mad at them for some perceived infraction they'd committed. This solution is still gleefully used by right wing gundamentalists today to excuse butting into everybody else's behavior, ostensibly to keep us from the wrath of god. But if evil is caused by bad human behavior, why do bad things happen to good people? Uh oh, back to inscrutability, the "Because I said so" of religious explanations. "Because I said so" is the go-to answer of the desperate, the last resort when a meaningful response is not available.

But then along comes Saul/Paul and thinks up this smiley face, sweet, loving god, because it's a much better sell: God loves you. You, personally! He's your own, personal imaginary friend. He *loves* you. All you have to do is love him back, follow the rules, and tithe to his church. This morphed into the all good, all powerful Christian god by preserving the Hebrew god's trait of being all powerful, and just adding the all-good, loving part. The early Christians comprehended the value of consistency and continuity with the older, more established tradition. They knew it was much easier to sell a new version of a trusted product than a whole new, unknown product. And make no mistake about it, god is a product and Paul was a salesman who really understood how to sell it.

Besides saving or doing something useful with your tithing money, what would be some other benefits of no religion? Well, 1) you could sleep in on Sundays, one of only two days off per week that most people have. So, you could spend your precious time on something worthwhile. Remember life is made up of time, so time is really all we have, making it the most precious commodity. 2) You would free yourself from the tyranny of the power structure created by religion- the rules keepers, cops, and religious authorities who tell you what you should do. 3) The Wizard of Oz thing; you could realize you had the answers within yourself the whole time. 4) You would experience the pride in accepting responsibility for yourself, being an evolved adult. 5) You might develop an internal locus of control, knowing what's right, without the erroneous cheat sheet that is religious doctrine. You know, a personal conscience. 6) You might learn to appreciate real-world miracles of nature, such as animals and trees and oceans, instead of waiting for the supernatural to occur. 7) Instead of using your brain to think about fairy tales which distract you from fear, you might use your brain for something more interesting, such as actual, reality-based ideas. 8) You might exercise your creativity fully instead of having it stunted by religion, which prefabricates everything for you. Sure, religion is believed to greatly inspire art, music, literature, and architecture, but wouldn't artists be even more creative without all the religious stencils that have been imposed on them- the monotonously multiple renderings of medieval saints, nativities, and Bible stories? Artists gonna make art.

Chapter 8- Afterword Stuff but a legitimate chapter you should not skip

I'm not a particularly persuasive person. I'm not a leader, but I'm definitely not a follower. I don't even understand the need to conform. I didn't concern myself with peer pressure, even as a teenager in high school. While I wasn't trying to fit in, I had lots of time and mental energy to think, and I figured a lot of things out. Presented here are lots of those things.

I know what I know. Not because I read it in a magic book, or an authority revealed it to me, or because I took it "on faith" from some learned sage. I know because I have spent my entire life working on figuring it out, observing, thinking about it, learning from mistakes, learning from and distinguishing what are reliable sources; in other words, building on knowledge, testing ideas, considering, and reconsidering information and experiences.

I also know what I don't know, what I haven't figured out, and I am able to live with that, while simultaneously not giving up. I know what I know. I know that men invented god to preserve and justify the masculinist system of competition that keeps us in eternal violence, hierarchy, hatred, war, and exploitation and in turn keeps us from evolving into a peaceful, enjoyable and ultimately happy world.

Even though I am right about a lot of things, I am obviously not infallible. I have not written all the answers herein. I'm just trying to provide a hopefully intelligent and somewhat entertaining boost on which to formulate reasonable philosophical improvements. For the love of reason, these musings must not be turned into dogma.

We have to get past this abjectly primitive waste of imagination that is religion. It is stifling us, keeping us from fulfilling our potential, and from meeting the goals of peace and plenty by keeping us masculinist and competitive. We *must* transition to a more cooperative form of global society or we will keep wiping ourselves out. Competition, as a universal system, **does not work**. Since god was such a bad idea, born of competition and fear, but eradicating violence and strife is a cherished goal, we need to all evolve and phase out god and competition, and phase in cooperation, reason, and fixing the food chain as our foundational principles.

Maybe it would help you to make this transition from religiosity by considering me a messenger (don't you dare say prophet), not from any mystical tradition, but who still has a necessary *metaphorical* communiqué from your *hypothetical* god.

He sent me to break up with you.

The first messenger western Yahweh sent was Moses. He sent him to tell you he liked you. Being a male god, he sent this bearer of his love declaration to you with a whole bunch of commands, requirements and thou shalts and shalt nots. Typical. Thou shalt have no other god before me (or in addition to me). He wants to be exclusive and will call you a whore if you dabble with others, but of course, he's still going to have 8 fucking BILLION others! Still, he makes you feel special. You're his chosen people. You can't resist.

Next, he sent Jesus to propose to you. If you love him, he'll offer you forever- eternal life together. Oh, and now his ex is a whore. Mary Magdalene. She didn't understand him. (Eye roll.) But you're Madge-Taylor-Green-stupid, and you accept the proposal. Dumb people cheer whenever you mention that your marriage has lasted for 2000+ years, as if it's an accomplishment, rather than just a bad habit.

Finally, he sent Muhammed. Muhammed was sent for your 635th anniversary to write you that beautiful poetry (the Qur'an), like a really spectacular greeting card, because god is too busy to get you a gift. He's busy. He's got a universe to run. He sent exquisite, flowery poetry! Isn't that enough? What the hell do you want from him? He's busy! And for another millennium and a half, it holds you, because *you love him* (said in a whiney, submissive voice).

But now, he's sent me (metaphorically! God is not real). He's breaking up with you via text message. He's asked me to tell you that he's tired of you. He finds you needy and clingy, and frankly, you've let yourself go. You're getting a little too old and wise for him. All you do is eat chocolate, dabble in science, and start wars. So, he's kicking you to the curb. He wants you to let him go. He knows what you're going to say: "But after all we've been through together! We've fought wars over you! Killed each other for you!" He wants you to know he appreciates it all, but it's time to move on. He'd like to say it's him, not you, but he can't-- it's you. You're smothering him. He can't breathe! The clinginess! The neediness!

And you keep growing the family! All those people to take care of! He's not sure he can do it anymore. All EIGHT FUCKING BILLION! Why'd you have to keep cranking out kids like cockroaches? Do you think resources grow on trees? Somebody has to work to make those resources! But how do you make enough for eight billion?! Come to think of it, you definitely ruined it, not him. He can leave with a clear conscience. This is all your fault. And he's found a younger, prettier, sexier, more naive species. So, just have some dignity and let go.

So, where does that leave you? The religious? The Gullible? Well, right now, you are going through the four stages of loss:

1) ***desperation and denial***. But we still love you. We can't live without you. This can't be happening. This only happens to other people. We'll kill ourselves!

2) ***anger and bargaining***. After all we've done for you! We gave you the best millennia of our existence! We can change. We'll quit eating so much chocolate and learn to settle differences by diplomacy, we swear! And science? Who needs it?

3) ***dawning independence***. This is kind of nice on our own. We can sleep in on Sundays and think through our own decisions.

4) ***We're over it***. What did we ever see in that creep? Everybody lives, happily, Atheistically, intelligently ever after!

Not yet convinced? OK, then. Look, you knuckle-dragging, mouth-breathing cave men, Jesus put me up to this. Turns out, he's an enlightened, ***WOKE*** guy who is appalled by all the superstition, divisiveness, and piety. And that goes for Allah, Baal, Buddha, Krishna, Odin, Vishnu, Yahweh, Zeus, Zoroaster, and all the rest of the pantheon.

Why do you think this got out? Even the gods are ready for you to grow out of Santa god, like your parents when you ostensibly believed in Santa until you were 12, and they had to keep gobbling up cookies on Xmas Eve and making big Santa footprints in the snow for you.

They all want you to let go and have faith in yourselves! You're like a 35 year old living in your parents' basement, sneaking to smoke weed and have sex. Let go!!!! Fly free, little birdies!!!

I'm doing you hayseeds a favor, exposing how your assorted imaginary religious figures really feel about you. They're trying to break up with humanity. They've done all they can do for you. You've just got to face reality and evolve. Now, just go!!!!

And don't shoot the messenger. Because if you do (and of course, I'm talking to you, violent trumpster trash gundamentalists), it just ***PROVES*** that you do not believe in god. Your all-powerful god doesn't need a lowly, deluded, pitiful, knuckle-dragging, mouth-breathing, demented wretch of a human like you to take care of an insignificant, little, gnat-like irritant like me. If you really believe in your omnipotent god, you know he's perfectly capable of smiting me himself, neither requiring nor desiring your agency in this matter. He could dramatically strike me with lightening! Would you deny your master his own revenge? If you think god needs *you* to get rid of me, you're treating god as though he's ***impotent***! If you think he needs you for this, your faith in him is nominal. So, you an Atheist!

Also, that's a fatwa, so you a Muslim! C'mon, Muslims, I've been fairly respectful of you, so no fatwas! I have in no way defamed Muhammed. I even spelled it correctly and praised his poetry.

In conclusion, all religions suffer from lack of credibility due to some form of the Problem of Evil (if god is all powerful and all good, how can evil exist?). They attempt to reconcile this fatal error by claiming that god is inscrutable and humans bring evil upon themselves via their own human behavior, despite bad things happening to good people. These untenable explanations are neither compelling nor convincing, like saying, "Because I said so!" is not instructive nor effective in child rearing. They are excuses that only a fanatic could believe (or pretend to believe).

The only plausible defense of the Problem of Evil is that the violent Food Chain was an error deliberately inserted into "creation" as a trick question for humanity to learn from, a test we have failed miserably. Our big, evolved brains failed us horribly; we didn't even interpret the problem appropriately as we greedily, violently, cruelly utilized the other animals for our own gluttonous desires, under supposed cover of having "dominion" over the other animals.

Now that religionists have this information, they must quit exploiting other animals (and other humans) or be exposed as not really believing in their various touchy-feely, smiley-face, feel-good traditions, all of which expect them to behave kindly. This is not just my opinion that you can pretend not to agree with. There is no other answer to the Problem of Evil. The inscrutability defense is a dubious solution that has no evidence or logic to back it up, the kind of defense one makes up when one has no defense, like a guilty defendant. Inscrutability is a pathetic excuse.

Conversely, the Food Chain Error fix has both circumstantial evidence and logic that's so tight, you can't think of a comparable quality explanation. The Food Chain is the worst possible ostensible "design", requiring murder and competition for survival, which in turn inculcates violence as a permanent necessity, the supposed "natural order of things", rendering every human problem on Earth unsolvable. The Food Chain is the foundation of all Earth's ills. You fix the food chain and you fix the Problem of Evil. You become a cooperative species rather than a competitive one and you fix the world. And we haven't even begun to consider this essential imperative.

How did it take over 5000 years for us to realize this simple, easy coup de grace of the religious version of god? It's so simple! It's the Food Chain, Stupid! (Thank you, James Carville, with or without your approval.)

You're either Vegan or you're Atheist. You can't ignore god's clear wishes for harmony as per Isaiah 11:6-8 and 65:25. (And Atheists, you can't ignore the nearly herbivorous propensities of our nearest evolutionary antecedents.) Evolving from crude competitive, survival-instinct, fear-based, reptilian-brain behavior to advanced cooperative, altruistic brain behavior is the only way to transcend our little Hell-heaven.

Chapter 9 - Speculations* on the Metaphysical Nature of Existence and Reality

*(NOT information, NOT facts, NOT dogma, and definitely NOT secret, esoteric revelations)

Brain vs. Mind. Our brain is matter. It is completely formed by, made of, dependent upon matter. When our matter passes from existence as in death, our brain will cease to exist. And thus, apparently everything it knew will cease to be known by it. But perhaps, our mind is energy. Physicists assert that energy never ceases to exist. That could mean our minds never cease to exist. But where do they go after the matter they appear to be housed in goes away, and do they maintain their knowledge and identity as an entity? We have zero evidence of this.

Also, some physicists have begun to assert that existence, indeed reality are both generated by mind and do not exist independently of mind. That there is no physical reality in the traditional sense we know it, but that we are all just making it up as we go along, as it were, with our minds. How fucking mind-blowing is that? It was very hard for me to even consider at first. I thought it was some airy fairy, hippy dippy, philosophical mumbo jumbo from someone who just wanted to sound deep. And it sounded suspiciously like a god argument to me. And you know me, I'll brook no flirtations with that sexist, arrogant sonofabitch, god! So, I have dismissed it since it began being floated.

But since I've been old, something has shifted. I have always fantasized about a possible ideal future. It's my hobby. It's my pleasurable mental exercise, like walking was my pleasurable physical exercise. It was just something I did for enjoyment, like reading a good book or watching a good show. But when you get old, uh oh, your future is death. It just is. We all pretend we can still have romance, activity, achievement when we're old, and we can have some of those things, but let's face it, our life's work is over. We've fallen in love, raised our usually too many kids, had our career, and our work is done. Hey old people, there's nothing wrong with feeling finished, especially if you're satisfied with your life. This is our vacation time- we can do whatever we want if we're fortunate enough to retire. We can relax!

Since I can no longer dream up a perfect future where I get to fall madly in love, be appreciated for and financially supported by my writing and travel the world giving lectures on my vast body of intellectual philosophy of life (like I was hoping for!!!) I am forced to think up something else cool to fantasize and cogitate about in order to continue pursuing my favorite activity. So, since death is my future, I have switched my focus to what happens to us after we die. Is it even possible to transcend matter and retain an individual identity as a release of energy? (NOT a "soul"!) We know our matter isn't going anywhere but back into the Earth in one form or another. But does our energy get to go somewhere and does it go as us or just as random energy in the universe? Or does it also just get recycled on Earth? We have no idea.

We can consider it, using information from flying dreams. Dreams are beyond our control, which is what makes them interesting and potentially contain information beyond what we perceive in physical reality. When you are flying in a dream, it feels so good. But we understand that our body could not possibly be with us in them (the physics of weight, lift, etc). It's grounds for wondering if perhaps there isn't some essence of ourselves that could exist outside our bodies, our matter.

Being a proper Atheist who didn't want to hear about souls and going to Jesus and all that hocus pocus, I was horrified by this discovery, after a flying dream one night, and am still skeptical. So, I processed that info in the only way I know how, and I have thought about it for several intervening decades. It was during this time that we began to hear about physicists claiming that there is no objective reality, that it is all generated by thought. It's almost like a dream. I *really* resisted this notion, because it was a little too magical for my tastes. This is a word we use to insult religionists.

Then I read that whatever we think about, we are experiencing (sorry, again no attribution because it was just some random reading, but hey, claim it if it's yours). And I was wary again, as one should be. But I noticed that just thinking about pleasant things, does make you experience pleasure. It's one of the techniques I used to keep me calm when I took the GREs for grad school. When I would be between sections of the test, I would take myself to the beach and listen to the waves and pretend to feel the sun on my skin and it would keep me from panicking or second guessing all my answers. So, we can definitely manifest different realities in our minds. But is that anything other than fantasy?

I have A LOT of experience with fantasy. When confronted with drudgery in my life (and I had less than most people, as I had no children and no spouse to deal with, but I did have to work for a living), I removed myself to my fantasies as frequently as possible. I was one of those proverbial people who would rather fantasize about playing Carnegie Hall than practice my scales (or in my case, fantasize about discussing my latest book on Letterman, rather than writing the damned book). When I would remove myself to my fantasies, I would in a sense be creating a perfect reality with my mind. I could make those "realities" feel very real to the point that they felt very good. I am not talking about sex, so get your minds out of the gutter.

Whatever we can think up, we can feel. Whatever we feel, we experience. Therefore, when we fantasize, we create new situations to feel. They might not appear before us in the concrete world of matter, but they are manifested in our minds and they make us feel them, so they have a mental and psychological reality. Thus, we *can* create reality to that extent.

Look, full disclosure, I don't know what the hell I'm talking about here. I have no particular knowledge nor expertise in the field of Physics or indeed any natural science, so I cannot do anything but speculate, hypothesize and cogitate on this subject. If you happen to think my contemplations are logical and maybe worthwhile, then by all means ruminate about them yourself. Do not assume they are correct, they very well may not be. (Remember, I'm just an old person trying to understand what comes next, if anything.) Maybe you'll think up something different, opposing and more reasonable, and have facts and logic to back up your conclusions. Great. Add to the body of knowledge. Maybe you'll have knowledge that I don't have which can back up some of my deliberations better than I can. Contemplate them if you find them interesting, just don't take them as received truth. Accept that they are mere conjecture and may well be wrong.

About 80% of the time, I appear to be doing nothing. At least 90% of that time, I **am** doing something, I'm thinking. We tend to think of thinking as "doing nothing". But while it's true that I am not using much physical energy at all, I am expending a great deal of mental energy. It's OK to be using mental energy instead of physical energy. One does not always have to be in motion to be accomplishing something. Ideally, we use both physical and mental energy. I sure don't use as much physical energy as mental, and it appears that some people don't use as much mental energy as physical. I have often thought that if I had had as much physical energy as I had mental energy, I would rule the world. (And it would be a much better place, because I would transition it to a Feminist Cooperative system!)

In fact, it would be a better world if more people spent more time using mental energy to think things through, rather than physical energy to say, engage in martial activities, or participate in sports, which are merely games and of very little consequence in the scheme of things. It's great to be physically healthy as demonstrated by athletic endeavors, but it's at least as important to be mentally healthy, which allows us to treat each other kindly. Intelligent, mentally healthy people are kind and loving, not hateful and frightened.

Did you know there was a Mind Olympics for a few years? I suspect most people haven't heard of them.

But the physical Olympics are all pervasive when they're happening, you can't get away from them. It shows you how much our primitive species values physical prowess over mental prowess. Think it has anything to do with men's priorities because of their physical advantage?

Just like you have to exercise your body to maintain physical health, one MUST exercise one's mind in order to be mentally healthy. Receiving "information" passively without thinking about it is worse for the mind than just sitting around eating bon bons all day is for the body. This is why cult members are mentally ill. They have to be snapped out of their cognitive torpor to recover. Unfortunately, this often requires a major catalyst, like a defeat in war (as in the case of the nazis), exposure and elimination of the leader (as in the case of the Warren Jeffs child molestation religious cult), or death (as in the Jim Jones and Heaven's Gate religious cults).

Reading is good mental exercise, depending on what you read. Even formulaic genre fiction can provide food for thought, if you follow up on it mentally, but if you read or watch entertainment without thinking about it, just reacting and feeling all the time, it's just empty mind calories, like the bon bons.

What the fuck do so many people have against contemplating the meaning of life???!!! Trying to figure out the best way to live life is the best mental exercise of all, but so many of us passively receive and accept what is spoon-fed to us by our families, communities, and societies. Don't let your parents do your homework, you won't learn anything!

Speculations are guesses, hypotheses, preferably educated guesses, but guesses all the same. And I can't stress enough that when I discuss ostensible afterlives and metaphysical reality, I am merely making guesses based on things I have read and experienced in my life without the requisite natural science credentials to prove any of what I'm saying. Maybe you are a physicist who can offer arguments and evidence for or against my assertions. Good. Welcome. I don't need to be right, I would be content with merely helping to move the conversation in a useful direction.

Anyway, we are composed of matter and energy. We definitely cease to exist in matter form. The evidence is quite conclusive. I don't even care. I'm mad at my body for betraying me with arthritis, like all old people should be at some point, and gratefully welcome death. (By the way, the argument that old age infirmity should make the elderly more receptive to death would have been a good "design" feature to argue for the existence of intelligent design, but y'all missed it in your fanatical fear of going to Jesus!) But I'm here to tell you, life ends. You gotta wrap it up.

Just like a book's got to have an ending, your life has to have an ending, too. And you should welcome it like a graduation or retirement. Death is just the completion of a project, *your* project. We must quit clinging to life like scared children and face whatever's next, even if it's nothing.

We should only stay alive as long as we are enjoying it. When a person starts waking up every morning wondering why they did so, it's time to go. Now, mind you, I'm not suggesting that anyone but the person themselves make that decision, I'm just saying when we're ready to call our project complete, we should be able to access a quick, painless death without judgment.

So, the question is, do we continue to exist as individual entities or consciousnesses after our matter dies? If we don't, that would mean our matter defines our individuality. Our bodies would be the most important element of our identities as it is all that holds it together. Can that be? It seems so base. But it could be. Does our energy connected to that body then just splinter and scatter into the wider universe where our consciousness is diffused, which is ceasing to exist as we care about it? Or does our energy just stay on Earth and convert to other beings, like our matter clearly does? I don't know. Neither do you. That's what makes it such a fun puzzle or mystery to figure out. You miss all the fun when you are convinced to stop at some pat dogma that offers all the answers, like an erroneous cheat sheet. It's a joy to exercise your mind on a fascinating question, but you can't experience that if you let your mind atrophy on religion.

Religion and romantic love seem to be two human constructs that are used for fear control and security. Religionists stick to their mythical hero despite all the evidence proving his lack of efficacy, just like women stick to their partner despite all the evidence proving his inability to love the way women want to be loved. Even in the face of harm being done to them by their loyalty, religionists and lovers cannot be dissuaded from their devotion.

In addition to security, love and religion seem to us to give our lives purpose. They are the best we are able to do to give meaning to our lives! Religion and love, fake as they may be, make us feel the kind of happiness one feels at a crowded amusement park, waiting in long, hot lines, sweating, with screeching kids all around, some of whom are your responsibility, all of which is costing you more than you can afford. Yet, you cheerfully go time after time, believing you are having a good time.

So, all religion and love do is make you fake happy because they make you feel like your life has purpose and meaning. But does it?

Religionists think that going to join god after death gives their life purpose. But why? What are they going to do there for eternity? Sit at the feet of Jesus and listen to his pearls of wisdom? For eternity? Remember how long that worked when you fell in love? Two days, two months, if you were lucky two years? Then you'd heard everything Honeybunch had to say and you just wanted them to shut the fuck up. So, how does being with god for eternity give your life meaning? Please explain and elucidate on your answer. That's religion down, as far as giving life purpose.

OK, so eternal life with god doesn't give life meaning, but your life's work gives it that purpose we all crave. You leave something behind for the world. For most people, it's just their progeny. How much meaning does that give your life? My great great grandmother, Alida Vandervoort was born a mere century before me. I never knew her and I knew extremely little about her, even though I knew a few older people who had known her. But they never talked about her. Except for an inane paper trail I discovered while doing genealogy, all traces of her, her life, and her identity are gone. Vanished. Irretrievable. As though she'd never been here. That's progeny down, as far as giving life meaning.

Unfair, you cry! What about people who leave more than kids? Great artists, musicians, philosophers, scientists? Tchaikovsky, Lao Tzu, Galileo? Their contributions are still remembered and affecting us today! *That* has meaning! OK, I'm willing to stipulate to that with one caveat. Of the approximately 16 billion who have ever lived (sorry, can't cite the source, was some random website, but let's just go with it, because the correct number isn't really what's important), how many of those significant characters are there? How many people even manage to leave any kind of lasting professional legacy for even a century? So, how does that miniscule fraction of the population confer meaning on the 16 billion humans who have ever lived? Congratulations to the rest of us- we are all just superfluous flotsam and jetsam in a sea of humanity.

Until… we find our purpose in life, our raison d'etre (reason for being), that which we must do to fulfill our contribution to existence. For me, it's my writings. I don't care that I won't be famous for it or even "successful" with it in my lifetime. I don't care that I'm not a household name like Jesus or Socrates, because I know for a fact that both of those guys were usurped and exploited by insincere people with nefarious agendas of their own. And that would just piss me off! I'd be OK with being an obscure thinker whose contribution was passed down through the ages and gradually made any impact on the building body of knowledge, while undergoing the least misinterpretation and misuse, rather than being a zeitgeist which is exposed to every crackpot and con man, and inevitably perverted.

People who are in the process of fulfilling their purpose can never compromise. They cannot choose anything, not fame, not fortune, not even survival, over their purpose. The purpose must go on! They cannot bend, bow, and compromise to commercial interests. Artists always seem driven to their purpose, more than most people, I think, but they are highly susceptible to commercial contamination.

I never met him or saw him perform while he was alive and didn't even discover him until after his death, but from observing his career via You Tube, I am guessing it's why Russian opera singer Dmitri Hvorostovsky couldn't go off on a tangent and become a filthy rich pop star, even though he had the looks and talent; it seems he had to spend his time, energy and superlative voice showcasing certain beloved Russian music for posterity and he seemed to instinctually know that was his purpose in life. He did it without wavering and seemed to step it up when he found out he had cancer. Look him up on You Tube, your loss if you don't.

He was an unsurpassed baritone who seemed musically uncompromised and was quite admired but not to the point where he lost all privacy, which could have distracted him from his mission, which he accomplished. A good thing, too, because look at the state of Russia now. We need their distinctive, culturally specific music preserved to remind the world of the ethnic beauty of Russian culture in this time of ruination. Russian music is outstanding, like their architecture. They have songs celebrating Russian fields, songs thanking their hearts for allowing them to love, and songs about flying away on the wings of the wind.

Russians are quite splendidly artistic, a fact that is hard to remember as the beady-eyed, little troll, putin turns their majestic country into a fascist, repressed dictatorship where only the stupidest, ugliest people are permitted to thrive. That will happen in the U.S. now that trump has been re-installed, and then it will spread to the whole world, because drunk with their success, the greedy men who back republicans and other fascists will buy up elections throughout Europe. Presto, chango, you're living in a new Dark Ages. There will be nowhere to hide from the kakistocracy (government by the worst people) and plan a revolution to a better system, with all the electronic surveillance available to them. Europe will fall, Africa will be kept divided under psycho warlords and Asia will be dominated by the Chinese dictatorship.

South America will be kept corrupt and powerless. Good luck finding any refuge. I plan on being dead.

What's going to happen to all of us, if anything, after death? Quite possibly nothing. That will be a letdown, but we won't be around to feel it, so… who cares? That's what eternal rest is. Not so bad, except you might remain here on Hell-heaven (Earth), endlessly reconstituting by nourishing and rematerializing as new Earthlings. Then you'd still be endlessly stuck experiencing Earth's worst case scenarios- a plant being hit by a lava flow, a tree being gashed by a lightning strike, a squirrel being devoured by a hawk, a horse being blown up in battle, a human dying of cancer. That is literally my worst case scenario of afterlives. That is the No Fun Afterlife, and possibly the most probable one. It's certainly the only one we can prove now.

Humans seem to instinctively know that our bodies (our matter) do not define us or our individuality. So, what does? It has to be our mind. Not our brain, which is matter and perishable, but our mind, which may be energy. Our minds define our selves. That's why people look at a corpse, and say, "She's not there, anymore. That's not her." But where is she? Her energy doesn't die with her matter, according to physicists, but is her mind stored in the energy left behind after shedding matter (death)? We do not know. If thought or mind is the energy that creates all reality and being, then thought creates the individual, and when energy is released from matter it seems as though it should convey the mind with it and preserve the individual entity contained in that mind, all of its knowledge, experience and personality. Or why did we go through all the trouble of learning all our lives?

Perhaps, it is energy's inability to rest or stop that keeps the world existing, like the movement of molecules. The mind cannot stop because it is energy, it is always thinking, which creates realities, so the constant expense of energy to think up reality keeps reality real, keeps it concrete like matter, not ethereal like a dream. Thought energy keeps the molecules moving to create matter. Proponents of meditation may disagree, but let them write their own thesis.

I am sick to death of being matter. It's cumbersome, heavy to carry around, and it requires constant maintenance! Organisms use up most of their energy just maintaining their matter: nutrition, hygiene, hydration, shelter, conveyance… constant fucking maintenance! It leaves very little energy to self actualize and attempt to manifest perfection!

Do we really have to stay on this rock repeatedly reconstituting as other beings on this petty Hell-heaven planet until it gets absorbed into a black hole millions of years from now, explodes and we dissipate? Ugh! I object! But that won't change it, if that's the case. I can object 'til I'm purple. I can even invent alternatives and believe in them with all my heart and soul, and it won't make a bit of difference.

But right now, here at the end of my life, when I'm SO tired, what is left to do in this puny Hell-heaven world but construct better ones with my mind? It's either that or storm the palace, and it's not quite time for that yet.

I hope these ruminations don't seem so speculative and supernatural that it calls into question the factuality and historicity of the preceding chapters. Maybe I'm just trying to model how to objectively approach contemplation of the unknown without using or creating dogma.

Epilogue

We will never eradicate the violence that keeps this world a living, fucking Hell without:

1) Eliminating the foundational violence that defines life on Earth, that is the food chain,

2) Replacing competition (the cause of violence) with cooperation, and sharing resources equitably.

That's just common sense! Don't let the greedy and powerful distract you from that fact with their shiny objects, such as gods, prayers and impossible promises of eternal life. Good leaders advocate critical thinking over obedience, so think. It's the only path to progress. We can't keep doing the same inefficacious thing we've been doing for tens of thousands of years and expect it to work. You know that's supposedly the definition of madness, right?

Scientists assert that we evolved these relatively big, sophisticated brains so that we could become aware of the universe and how it works. But I submit that these brains also evolved so that we could figure out how things **should** work and make the necessary improvements, not just technologically, but even more importantly philosophically, psychologically and sociologically.

This world isn't worth living in, as is. We must fix it. The constant struggle for survival and the fragility of our welfare are like a sledge hammer hanging precariously over a doorway or a game of Russian roulette. You never know when the hammer will drop or the bullet will fire. Look at both the Russians and Ukrainians. They were going along happily, finally enjoying some freedom and prosperity, and then bang! A male psychopath took it away, just like that.

We have to evolve. We need a quantum leap in human evolution, like right now, or I fear humans won't be around permanently. We've got psychopaths with nukes, a looming global kakistocracy of small-penised, insecure pedophiles, and a rapidly dying planet.

We have not developed the brain sophistication we need for this point in human history, because *under male rule, we've expended the vast majority of our brain power on technology to fight with each other and compete*, instead of learning to pull together to progress as a world community, like we should have done. We value gadgets and toys more than we value social and mental health. Just like getting sex all wrong for millennia may have stunted our sexual evolution, *getting our social behavior all wrong since the beginning of our existence has stunted our brain evolution*. Now we *must <u>re-wire our brains</u>* to use reason and cooperation to focus on resolving the myriad problems we face, which threaten our very existence. We must learn to exclude superstition (religion) and competition from the administration of humanity.

Competition is for athletics, and not even necessary for that. Many games can be played cooperatively; for example, volleyball can be played by scoring how many volleys the two sides can cooperate to keep the ball from hitting the ground. On a committee to plan a work retreat once, I suggested using cooperative activities, and a male colleague stated he couldn't see the point if nobody won!

When I play the board game "Life" with friends and family, we refuse to play for money and instead proclaim the winner to be the happiest player at the end. Our rules allow for participants to choose whether they want to get married, have children, and substitute pets for offspring. My (female) friend once just gave me $100,000 when I went broke during a game. My nephew was bothered by these alterations and could only think of winning as the traditional way of accumulating the most wealth. He was aghast at not following "the rules". (Even though, following the rules in real life will usually leave you poor and exploited, and an ostensible loser.)

I'm not saying there can be no friendly competition. Competition is healthy for motivation, but our main impetus should be improving the common good, with personal gain secondary. And again, as stated previously, remuneration should stay within reasonable parameters of how variable the possible worth of human work can be. Elon Musk's and Jeff Bezos' work is not that much more worthy than yours and mine because nobody can be that much better than someone else. It's simply not possible. It's injustice, because they have more than they deserve.

All our problems are interconnected- sexism, racism, classism, religionism, specieism, nationalism, tribalism. We can't fix one and not the others, because that won't solve anything. We must resolve them all. The common denominator is violence and competition, so that is the starting point- replace competition with cooperation, and eliminate the foundational violence (the food chain) by ceasing to kill. The good news is, there happens to be a group on our planet who possess just the right skills to lead this paradigm shift- *women*. Women must take the lead on this. Men have failed and will continue to fail.

In case you haven't noticed, men have had unchallenged, unobstructed power to govern for all of human existence, and all they have ever wrought is violence, war, oppression, chaos, cruelty, and political strife. They have not solved our problems in 30,000+ years of having power, so they have failed spectacularly at governance, and it is time for them to step aside. Or more realistically, be pushed aside, as they cannot seem to relinquish power gracefully (think of all the elderly republicans who completely compromised their values over trump threatening to primary them- they could have retired comfortably and worked from the sidelines, but they couldn't stand to lose their power, and chose to become morally bankrupt toadies, and now they are dying in this state, with no redemption possible anymore).

This millennia-long history of ***Male Governance Failure*** (***MGF***) proves that they should not be leaders in government, because they clearly cannot handle power and they cannot solve political problems without violence. They are too emotional, too hysterical (or rather gonadical) to govern. They are too full of toxic testosterone. When they get upset, they fight, threaten, and often resort to mass violence. We have 30,000 years of proof of ***the fact that men have failed at governing***. There is no period of history that has been free of violence, scarcity, and exploitation. Think about that.

If men had been successful leaders, we would be living in a just, prosperous, happy world right now. **They have _never_, not once, succeeded at governing well. They have a 100% failure rate over 30,000 years!!!**

And if you think democracy was an example of success, ask poor and minority people if they think we were ever well governed. Men always select groups to exclude from prosperity, so that there are people who must do the hardest work for the least material gain. Democracy has been no different. You might argue that creating democracy was some kind of pinnacle of governance success. But what destroys democracy? Competition. What is causing the U.S. constitution to be systematically dismantled by the trumpster trash? Greed. Competition for wealth. Not even democracy can work in a competitive system.

Men are good at making and building stuff with their large, muscular bodies and figuring out technological gadgetry with their shrewd, competitive minds, so that's where they should utilize their talents. They should not be heads of state, CEOs, directors, or managers. They cannot handle power over other people. The good ones can be allowed to be consultants only, in management and government.

The masculinist competitive system is *never* going to work. That has been proven over tens of thousands of years. From tribal warlords to protector kings to democracy, the masculinist competitive system has always failed, by letting power and wealth acquisition consistently override the common good.

If an organization had an employee who failed to successfully perform their job, failed to solve the most rudimentary problems, and even did major damage, that employee would be fired. It is impossible to deny the pattern of complete failure of male rule over 30 millennia. Why have we let these bunglers rule for so long? How have we not been screaming from the rooftops about ***Male Governance Failure*** for decades, even centuries? All male rulers ever do is get people killed. It's happening right this second!

Ironically, the male system of socialization of women that requires them to be stewards of families, also makes women better governors. Women learn to cooperate, compromise, and solve novel problems in order to sustain their families. Women are socialized to be nurturing, so they are more likely to prioritize hungry children over profits, sentient beings over shiny rocks. My sister remarked that if women were in power instead of trump and netanyahu, there would be no starving, freezing, homeless, wounded or dead children in Gaza, because women could not stand for that. ***Male indoctrination of women to be good mothers and wives has inadvertently made women better leaders than men.***

Perhaps countries should be run like families, not businesses.

The reason you'll never get men to govern correctly is because they are never going to give up competition as their guiding principle. They consider cooperation effeminate, and they rank femininity beneath masculinity. Competition *requires* ranking. There have to be winners and losers, and men are terrified of being identified as effeminate, because it threatens their masculine sense of superiority, of being the winners.

Now, men, let me reassure you. I know the idea of women taking over governance scares you, because people tend to assume others think and act like themselves. But we will not do to you what you have done to us. We will not exploit you, hurt you, make you second class citizens, or commit violence against you. We will not compete with you. We want to cooperate with you to make the world and life better for our offspring and ourselves to enjoy.

We love you. (We're just very disappointed in you.) We want to enjoy our lives with you. We don't hate you, like you appear to hate us. You can trust us, even though we couldn't trust you. We will just not put up with your toxically masculine bullshit anymore. Life will be better, I promise. We **can** do better.

We can love and enjoy you without placing you beneath us. We are happy with equality and can teach you to be. You **will** be happier than you are now, with all your male loneliness epidemic, which you blame on women not being sufficiently subservient. Good god, how did you ever get it all so wrong? Let us fix it.

Best not to fight us on this, because if push comes to shove and you force us to get rid of all of you (like, by prying your guns from your cold, dead hands? OK.), that will be no sweat to us, because comedian/writer/actor Brett Goldstein has already agreed to be kept on as a mascot, do the cooking and cleaning, and never expecting sex (he claims), promises to meet any reproductive needs we might have by leaving "a lit'tle pot' o' cum" whenever necessary. (Now, we know he really expects to be getting lots of sex, because he's so handsome people actually thought he was CGI, but what he doesn't know, because he has no experience with it, is that he will be too exhausted from all the "women's work" to want all that sex.) And like women who do all that "women's work", plus their jobs, we'll still expect Brett to continue to do stand-up, write great entertainment, and act in TV and films, so we can all enjoy his ridiculously good looks. Then, when he's done with all that, we'll ask if he wants to be **banged.**

In conclusion, it will take a rare major paradigm shift, but we have no choice. We must shed masculine religion and competition and transition ASAP to feminine reason and cooperation. That's the quantum leap we need to survive. Continued competetiveness leads inexorably to global serfdom to billionaires, most of whom seem to be rapists and pedophiles. Good Luck.

The End?

Bibliography

Armstrong, Karen, **Jerusalem**, 1996, Ballantine Books, NYC.

Bloom, Harold & Rosenberg, David, **The Book of J**, 1990, Grove Weidenfeld, NYC.

Crown Publishers, Inc., **The Lost Books of the Bible**, 1979, Gramercy Books, NYC (originally published 1926 World Publishing Co. from 1820 William Hone collection titled The Apocryphal New Testament).

Eisenman, Robert, **James, the Brother of Jesus**, 1997, Penguin Books, NYC.

Finkelstein, Israel & Silberman, Neil Asher, **The Bible Unearthed**, 2001, The Free Press (Simon & Schuster), NYC.

Fredriksen, Paula, **Jesus of Nazareth, King of the Jews**, 1999, Vintage Books (Random House), NYC.

Freke, Timothy & Gandy, Peter, **The Jesus Mysteries**, 1999, Harmony Books (Crown Publishing), NYC.

Friedman, Richard Ellliot, **Who Wrote the Bible?,** 1987, Harper Collins, San Francisco.

Golb, Norman, **Who wrote the Dead Sea Scrolls?**, 1995, Touchstone (Simon & Schuster), NYC.

Halo Press, **The Missing Books of the Bible, Vols I II**, 1996, Halo Press, Baltimore, MD.

Kirsch, Jonathan, **The Harlot by the Side of the Road**, 1997, Ballantine (Random House), NYC.

Klassen, William, **Judas, Betrayer or Friend of Jesus?,** 1996, Augsburg Fortress Press, Minneapolis.

Lamsa, George, translator, **Holy Bible from the Ancient Eastern Text**, 1933, AJ Holman Co (now Harper Collins), NYC.

Marcus, Amy Dockser, **The View from Nebo**, 2000, Little, Brown & Co., Boston.

Pagels, Elaine, **The Gnostic Gospels**, 1979, Vintage Books (Random House), NYC.

Robinson, James M., Ed., **The Nag Hammadi Library**, 1990, Harper Collins, NYC.

Ryan, William & Pitman, Walter, **Noah's Flood**, 1998, Touchstone (Simon & Schuster), NYC.

Schonfield, Hugh, **The Passover Plot**, 1965, Element, Inc., Rockport, MA.

Sheehan, Thomas, **The First Coming**, 1986, Dorset Press, NYC.

Silberman, Neil Asher, **The Hidden Scrolls**, 1994, The Berkley Publishing Group, NYC.

Stanton, Elizabeth Cady, **The Woman's Bible**, 1999, Prometheus Books, Amherst NY, (originally published 1898, European Publishing Co., NYC).

Thiering, Barbara, **Jesus and the Riddle of the Dead Sea Scrolls**, 1992, Harper Collins, NYC.

Thompson, Thomas L., **The Mythic Past**, 1999, Basic Books, London.

Vermes, Geza, **The Complete Dead Sea Scrolls in English**, 1962, Penguin Books, NYC.

Wise, Michael O., **The First Messiah**, 1999, Harper Collins, NYC.